# STEP BY STEP THROUGH

# MODERN SQUARE DANCE HISTORY

## JIM MAYO

ISBN: 1-4140-0502-4 (e-book)
ISBN: 1-4140-0503-2 (Paperback)
ISBN: 1-4140-0504-0 (Dust Jacket)

Library of Congress Control Number: 2003096882

This book is printed on acid free paper.

Printed in the United States of America
Bloomington, IN

1stBooks – rev. 11/14/03

# DEDICATION

This book is dedicated to my most loyal fan. JoAnn has shared more than forty years of my square dance experience. Her praise has been generous and her criticism gentle - and necessary. She encouraged this project as she has everything I have undertaken. No caller could have a better partner.

# CONTENTS

Acknowledgments ................................................................ vii

Introduction ........................................................................ ix

Chapter 1  -  The Traditional Environment ................................. 1

Chapter 2  -  Square Dance Popularity Explodes........................ 15

Chapter 3  -  Choreography In The 1950's ................................ 27

Chapter 4  -  The Growth Of Clubs And Festivals ..................... 37

Chapter 5  -  Choreography Changes........................................ 47

Chapter 6  -  New Calls And Choreography Management ........... 55

Chapter 7  -  The New Call Flood............................................ 63

Chapter 8  -  Caller Training.................................................. 69

Chapter 9  -  Club Life Is Rich .............................................. 77

Chapter 10 -  1970 - Things Are Changing ............................... 81

Chapter 11 -  The CALLERLAB Era Begins .............................. 93

Chapter 12 -  1974 - 1980 A Period Of Rapid Change............... 117

Chapter 13 -  Square Dancing Is Everywhere........................... 127

Chapter 14 -  All Position Dancing, An Elusive Goal ............... 139

Chapter 15 -  Dancing Changes ............................................. 149

Chapter 16 -  Problems Get Our Attention .............................. 163

Chapter 17 -  Solutions Are Proposed .................................... 175

Chapter 18 -  The New Millennium Arrives - Where Are We?.... 189

Chapter 19 -  A Subjective Summary ..................................... 195

# ACKNOWLEDGMENTS

While I have lived through and been an active part of the entire history described in this book, it is by no means a product of my sole effort. I expected, when I began, that I would sit at my trusty keyboard and transfer my memories into print. I learned in the first dozen pages that my memory was both incomplete and imperfect. Fortunately, ours is an activity that develops friendships and I have benefitted from those repeatedly during the creative process. These friends have been both contributors and critics but their participation has been motivated, always, with the kind of warmth and goodwill that is taken for granted in the square dance community.

The late Bob Osgood is, without a doubt, the most prolific writer in the square dance world. His monthly magazine is the chronicle of modern square dancing before 1985. He was quick to grant my request to quote extensively both from the magazine and from his other writing. He has also been a helpful sounding board throughout the several years I have been working on this project.

Living only twenty miles from the Square Dance Foundation of New England facility in Manchester, New Hampshire has been wonderfully convenient. Their collection is both very complete and very well organized and presented. A small group of very dedicated people has worked very hard to establish and maintain that museum.

My writing has always suffered from the fact that my thoughts move more quickly than my fingers. Editorial and typographic errors are rampant even after I have rewritten and reorganized. While spelling and grammar checkers can correct some of these they lack compassion and the ability to distinguish and accommodate personal emphasis and style. Carleen Loper accepted the challenge and contributed substantially to the readability of this reminiscence.

I am pleased to have been able to write this history while many of the founding participants were still around to discuss it and share their memories. Most important among those to whom I went for such help were Al Brundage and Earl Johnston who have been my mentors and associates for more than five decades. In that league Bill Peters is a short-timer. We met in 1963 but we worked together very closely from then until he retired from active calling in the early 1990's. We were part of the founding group of CALLERLAB, taught callers together for twenty years, both chaired the Caller Training Committee and were major contributors to the CALLERLAB caller training *Technical Supplement* which is the most respected source of technical information about calling square dances. Throughout our association Bill and I have tested our thinking against the opinions of each other. His critical reading of my writing has been very helpful.

# INTRODUCTION

Square dancing has a long history. Humans have danced almost since the first beings stood on two legs. Rhythm was created by banging a stick on a hollow log or some other primitive means and, as soon as there was rhythm, people tried to match their movement to it. Dancing by groups of eight people arranged on the sides of a square can be traced back several centuries. This form of dancing came to North America with the earliest settlers and became part of the social life of both the United States and Canada. These earliest "square" dances were complete routines. They were learned by the dancers and danced without a caller. S. Foster Damon, in his book *Square Dancing, A History* published in 1957 suggested that the creation of the caller happened in the early 1800's. He also noted that some attempts to introduce this approach in England met with disdain. In the beginning callers were referred to as "prompters." Their job was to remind people of the steps of a dance routine they had learned.

The traditional form of square dancing continues to be popular and has changed little from the way it was done in the past. Traditional square dances are complete routines done in the same way each time they are danced. When dance routines pass from one caller to another they are sometimes modified. An individual caller, however, usually presents them without change each time they are done. The history of traditional square dancing has been well documented. Books that have been written about square dance history have, with few exceptions, made no distinction between traditional square dancing and what has come to be called modern western square dancing, even though the modern form of this recreation is significantly different from its traditional counterpart. This book will describe and define that difference. It will also trace the popularity of this new way of square dancing and the changes that have occurred as it continued to develop over the last fifty years.

Modern western square dancing has existed for only a brief period at the end of the centuries-long history of square dancing. The main path of development for "traditional" square dancing continues without interruption and with only minor change. The modern variation is different in significant ways. During the last half of the twentieth century its popularity and growth far outstripped that of its traditional parent. There are areas where traditional square dancing, or its sibling, contra dancing, is quite popular but it never experienced the wild growth of modern club square dancing. As we enter a new century that growth has faded and it is clear that the modern style of square dancing is experiencing difficulty. Many reasons are put forth to explain that difficulty. None of these, however, have been based on a thorough examination of the changes that have taken place in the dancing itself. I hope this history will help us better to understand those changes.

The most fundamental difference between traditional and modern square dancing is the changing of the dance routine as it is being danced. The details of that process and the nature, timing and extent of the change will fill a substantial portion of this book. It is clear that the idea of changing the dance routine did not happen over a short period of time. In fact, the ways in which the dance patterns are changed are still being modified today. There is a tendency among both dancers and callers to regard the activity as static. A casual look at history, however, quickly shows the error of such a view. Unfortunately, few in the modern square dance world have taken even a casual look at history. Perhaps this has been partly because no comprehensive historical document has been available. For most dancers and many callers, square dancing began the night they first walked into beginners' class. There has been no easy reference available to help them learn how square dancing became such an important part of their lives and that of so many other people. This book will be such a reference.

Another reason for me to undertake to document how we created the type of square dancing we call modern is that I have been active as a caller throughout the last half of the twentieth century. I learned to dance to one of the legends of traditional square dancing, Ralph Page, and was also introduced to the modern form of square dancing by one of the most popular and respected of the early modern style callers, Al Brundage. I have been involved in the formation of caller associations starting with my local Tri-State Callers Association and continuing to the New England Council of Caller Associations and The International Association of Square Dance Callers known as CALLERLAB. Most of the early, popular traveling modern callers were my personal friends. I was the editor of and one of the major contributors to the universally-accepted textbook and guideline for teaching callers, the *CALLERLAB Curriculum Guideline for Caller Training* and its *Technical Supplement.*

I am fortunate to live near the Square Dance Foundation of New England and have had unrestricted access to its facilities, including complete collections of *Sets in Order, American SquareDance* and *The New England Caller* (now *The Northeast Square Dancer*) magazines. When I began the process of writing this book, I assumed my involvement in the development of modern square dancing would allow me to write without the need to do extensive research. I was wrong. My memory was far too general. When it came to writing the details down on paper, I found I had to study carefully what others had written. I was constantly surprised by how early in the development of modern square dancing the fundamental changes occurred.

Throughout the book, I will often use examples from the New England area to illustrate the points I want to make; in part because my knowledge of events that took place in New England is far more detailed than what occurred in other areas. I am reasonably confident that changes that occurred were similar across North America. My general sense is that the first modifications began in California and then were copied in other areas starting, usually, with those that were most densely populated. By the early 1960's there were newsletters and note services that provide clues to the changes that were taking place. Before that, most information was passed by word-of-mouth. Most of the traveling callers who came through New England stayed with us as house guests.

I have not included definitions of square dance calls in the book except in the case of those that are no longer in regular use. Anyone who has completed a modern square dance teaching program will know the meaning of nearly all of the calls I have used in choreographic examples. The complete definition of all calls currently being used in the most popular programs of modern square dancing is available on the CALLERLAB Internet website, www.CALLERLAB.org.

There is not a great deal of documentation available on this subject. We were too busy having fun to spend time writing about it. The major exception is the *Sets in Order* magazine. Established in 1949, it became the principal chronicle of the modern western square dance activity. Its editor, Bob Osgood, has a keen sense of history and throughout its existence he made certain that major events and trends were described in its pages. *The Caller Text*, published by the magazine in 1985, was a collection of articles from its pages and is the closest thing to a history that we have had until now. *American SquareDance* magazine is also a valuable reference. Rickey Holden was a roving editor of that publication for a while and his travel writing contributed to the nationwide coverage. Willard Orlich became editor of the Workshop section of the magazine in 1962. Willard, although not a caller, was active in the development of a challenging form of modern square dancing. Stan and Cathy Burdick purchased that magazine from Arvid Olson in 1968. They were established participants in modern square dancing and included many articles that increase our understanding of the development of the activity.

Yet another reason, and probably the most important for me, to write about the creation and development of modern square dancing is the hope that we can learn from the past. I believe that square dancing is a wonderful recreation. As we begin the new century, its popularity is not spreading rapidly. This doesn't make square dancing unique. Changes that have taken place in our society and the pace of daily life have had an impact on many activities. Learning to square dance the modern way takes time and commitment. Busy young people of today seem to have a short supply of both. Instant gratification is the popular route. As I write this, there is a substantial effort underway by CALLERLAB to promote square dancing. Some of us believe that we have to make some changes in our "product" if it is to serve folks in the future as well as it has served us. One of the most wonderful aspects of this recreation is the friendships that are formed in square dance clubs. In our modern society social contact is not as usual and regular as it once was. Square dancing, particularly in groups that meet regularly, is a wonderful way to meet people.

# CHAPTER 1 - THE TRADITIONAL ENVIRONMENT

The modern form of square dancing is different from its traditional forbears in several significant ways. The differences will be easier to identify if the reader understands that traditional background. Square dancing has been an American folk dance since the earliest settlers arrived in North America. They brought with them dance forms from their countries of origin. These dances shared some common characteristics and often included four couples dancing together in a "set." The prompter or caller was a uniquely American innovation. No one has established why or exactly when but only in America were the dancers reminded of the dance action while they were dancing.

The fundamental qualities of square dancing have changed very little since the caller was added in the early nineteenth century. Its popularity ebbed and flowed as did its status in the social structure. It was an element of country life seen often at barn raisings and corn husking parties. It also appeared in higher social circles. In the middle of the 20th Century, the industrialist Henry Ford encouraged a spurt in the popularity of square dancing and an elevation of its social status. He invested a substantial personal wealth and interest in promoting it. A great deal has been written about the "Henry Ford" revival of square dancing in the 1920's and 1930's.

As the 1940's began, square dancing was available in a wide variety of settings. It was done by elite groups at the Wayside Inn in Massachusetts, by Ford Motor Company executives in the hall that Mr. Ford built for it in Dearborn, Michigan, by cowboys and their partners at barbeques in Texas and in community groups all over the country. Little changed as life got

1

back to normal after World War II. Many of the pre-war programs started up again. Traditional square dancing was a popular social recreation.

The styles of dancing and the styles of prompting varied greatly but there was some similarity in the dance routines. In his book *"Cowboy Dances,"* first published in 1939, Dr. Lloyd Shaw, who was a school principal in Colorado Springs and known to most as "Pappy" Shaw, described the origins of square dancing in the American West. He traced the heritage of that dancing back to two distinctly different origins. The Quadrille style was common in the northeastern United States and the Kentucky Running Set was danced in the mountain country of the U.S. Southeast.

The quadrille was quite a formal style of dance. It was done in the royal courts of France and came to the New World with the earliest settlers. The dance action in quadrilles, as the name suggests, involved a four-couple dancing group. Two opposite couples commonly executed a series of dance actions together. The same series of steps were then repeated by the other opposite pairs. These dance actions were followed by a series of steps involving all four couples at the same time. Many of these routines have been documented in the dance books of the early dancing masters. When these formal routines were adapted into the folk activities in the northern colonies, the pattern of two opposing couples working together was retained.

The other form of dancing that Dr. Shaw identified as a precursor of square dancing as he observed it in the Southwest was the Kentucky Running Set. The name Sicilian Circle is also used to identify this form of dancing. In it, a circle of two-couple sets is formed with couples in each set facing each other and with their backs to the couples in the adjoining set. Each series of dance actions ends with the couples passing by each other to face a new couple from the adjoining set.

Dance patterns that are common in traditional square dancing show evidence of these origins. The visiting couple routine, which was one of the standard forms, can be seen as a development from the Running Set. Couples were numbered in sequence to the right from the number one couple (with their back to the front of the hall.) The number one couple "visited" each couple in sequence around the square and repeated the same actions with each of them. The other common pattern in traditional square dancing involved the Head Couples doing a routine which was then duplicated by the Side Couples. There were regional variations in the numbering of the couples that also support the double heritage track. In areas where the Running Set heritage was strong, the couples were numbered in a counterclockwise rotation from number one. The Quadrille influence sometimes resulted in the Head Couples being numbered one and two while the Sides were number three - to the right of number one - and four.

Whatever the form of the dance, it was popular. Huge crowds were dancing in squares all over the United States and Canada. There were as many different styles and dance patterns as there were common features. Each had a set of dance patterns and they were done the same way, and often in the same order, at every dance. In the next state they might be slightly modified but from night to night there was very little change. Some callers were traveling away from their home area and they spread their own versions of the dance routines as they traveled. Dr. Shaw took a group of students from his Cheyenne Mountain School on tours across the United States. They demonstrated square dancing and spread the interest in it widely.

## EARLY DANCE STRUCTURE

A traditional evening of square dancing was divided into segments of dancing. These took several forms depending on the area and local practice. Some included both squares and contras[1] in the program and most had some form of couple dancing as well. A segment of square dancing was called a tip and could include two or three dance routines, each done to a different musical tune. In some areas there were patter calls and singing calls. In singing calls the caller followed the musical melody with his voice in delivering the dance directions and usually also sang words from the original song during the promenades. In patter calls the caller matched only the rhythm and, sometimes, the chord pattern of the music. When there were both patter and singing calls they often were arranged in sets of three with two singing calls separated by a patter call. Between tips the couple dances, collectively called round dances, took various forms. Waltzes and Polkas and ethnic folk dances such as the Schottische are examples of such round dances.

---

[1] Contra dance formation differs from the square that gives square dancing its name. The contra formation is two lines of dancers facing each other. Most of the dance actions are the same as those used in the square formation. The contra formation was common in Scottish and English dances and was a regular part of "square" dances in some areas.

Whatever the local format for a square dance, it varied little from one night to the next. A caller would likely use the exact same dance routines and the same music. Singing calls, in particular, did not vary from one night to the next. Nor, in fact, did singing calls change when they were done by another caller. There was a particular set of dance actions that fit each of the singing calls and all callers used the same actions with an individual tune. Learning to square dance involved attending a dance with experienced dancers. A newer dancer usually squared up in the number four position. In this way, the action could be observed before one was called on to participate. It was courtesy when forming squares to leave the number one position to be filled last.

Earl Johnston began square dancing in 1943 in Southern Connecticut. He shares his memory of his earliest experiences in this quotation.

It is interesting to note that 80% of the dancers were teenagers and for the most part attended on a regular basis, rarely missing. The dances were, for the most part, old traditional dances but they had deteriorated in content over the years...We didn't do Ladies Chains or Right and Left Thru as we know them today and as they were described in books like *Good Morning*. A Ladies Chain was called Ladies Change and the girls crossed over and did a regular swing for one or two times around and then on Change Back went home and repeated the swing with partner. A Right and Left Thru was even more convoluted. From a circle of four the quickest couple made an arch and the slower couple ducked thru the arch then both did what is now called a California Twirl. Then the slows made an arch and the quicks dove thru the arch and then another California Twirl. None of these things were ever taught. You just watched what the others did and aped their movements. It usually took two nights to become an expert.

We only did stars to certain songs. The most notable was Manana which in reality was Texas Star but no one knew it by that name. We did a dance called Jitterbug to the tune of Captain Jinks and it was probably the most popular dance of the evening. We did Spanish Caballero, Golden Slippers, Marching Thru Georgia, Duck for the Oyster, Wring Out the Old Dish Rag, The Basket, Grapevine Twist and many others I can't seem to recall. We always ended the evening with The Waltz Quadrille which was also a super simple dance but everyone enjoyed. We did lots of swinging 16 counts and

4

lots of swing in the center and six hands around, Kiss Her If You Dare.

The visiting couple format was one of the two that were most common in traditional square dancing. In this type of routine that Dr. Shaw believed developed from the Southern Mountain Running Set, the active couple visited each of the other couples doing the same dance action with each of them. Usually each of the couples' visits to all the others was followed by an action involving all four couples such as an Allemande Left, Grand Right and Left (which in those days went all the way around to the starting place.) These dividing actions were called the "break," which is a term that has remained in use although many now apply the term only to the routines that come at the opening, between the figures and at the end in a singing call.

The other standard format for traditional dances was the quadrille. In this type of dance the Head two couples did a dance action and then the Side two couples did the same action. This was followed by a "break" involving all of the dancers in the set and the actions were repeated. Earl Johnston, in the quotation above, says, "We only did stars to certain songs. One of these…in reality was Texas Star but no one knew it by that name." The star action was used little in New England traditional dancing and when it did appear it was usually part of the break.

Even traditional dancing has never been completely static. It is, after all, a folk activity and the "folk" have a way of changing things. Although I will identify changing dance routines as the most characteristic element of modern square dancing, it is clear that change was introduced into the traditional form as well. The only distinction in the earliest days of the separation of the modern from the traditional was a matter of degree.

The earliest variations involved changing the action in the quadrille format from the Heads to the Sides. The Heads did one of the standard routines and then a different standard routine was called for the Sides. It was a small step from that to changing the action in the visiting couple format each time a different pair of couples was involved. Another small variation involved both Head Couples doing a "visiting" type dance at the same time. Rather than saying "Number One Couple lead to the right and…" The caller said "Head Two Couples lead to the right…" There was less standing around watching other people dance. Al Brundage told me that the first variations he remembers were using a different dance action for each of the couples as they "visited" the others. Couple One would do Lady Round the Lady with each of the other three couples and then Couple Two would lead out to do the Duck for The Oyster routine with each of the couples they visited. It was possible to use three different dance actions for one couple. They did a different routine with each of the couples they visited.

All of these changes became possible in part because the sound equipment being used had improved so that dancers could actually hear and respond to the caller's variations of the routines they had learned. This changing of the dance routines during the dance is the principal distinction between traditional and modern square dancing. It began to spread as the popularity of square dancing grew right after the end of World War II. Realization that a dance routine could be changed while the dancers were doing it started a process that was to alter square dancing in very substantial ways. It was a step onto a path from which there was no turning back. No longer was square dancing something that you could learn in a few visits to a dance with experienced dancers. The variations meant that each program included many more dance actions than when a single dance action was used for each of the couples in the square.

A few callers started to travel, meeting callers from other areas from whom they learned of dance actions they had not seen before. Dr. Shaw took his student demonstration groups on the road and they showed patterns that were more intricate than those commonly in use. On these tours he promoted his summer square dance institutes and callers from many areas met there. They shared dances from their areas and learned new styles of dancing to take home with them.

Many saw the Allemande Thar routine for the first time at the Shaw gatherings. It had been developed by Dr. Shaw for use in his demonstrations as a complete routine inserted as "break" between repetitions of a visiting couple or quadrille dance. The call would have been delivered as: "Allemande Left for an Allemande Thar, Go forward two and the gents turn in to a back up star. Shoot that star to the heavens whirl, go right and left to the second girl. Then the men back in to another Thar. Shoot that star and swing your own then promenade." There would have been no variation in that whole routine - initially.

An interesting personal experience illustrates the tensions of the transition period. In the summer of 1949, I was dancing regularly to Ralph Page in the town halls of southwestern New Hampshire. He had attended the Lloyd Shaw institute and at one of the dances soon after his return he called the dancers through the Allemande Thar routine. I noted the change from his usual routines and asked him about it after that tip. He said he had just tried it out to see how it went - and added that he didn't think much of it. He never used it again.

Others were more receptive to change. Another action that spread, probably from the Shaw schools, was the Wagon Wheel. It was a break type of action involving a set routine following an Allemande Left from a basic square formation. Callers looking for ways to add variety to their program started to invent calls. An early instance of this happened at one of the Shaw schools. The name for the call Dos Paso was created by Dr. Shaw as a compromise. The "Texas" version of Docey Do was quite different from the back-to-back action of the Dos a Dos as it was done in the East. Although the action was not the same, the pronunciation was identical and this resulted in conflict among those who gathered in Colorado Springs. Shaw negotiated with Herb Greggerson that the hand-turn action of the Docey Do would be called Dos Paso in honor of its Texas origins. The long-term effect of this compromise has been the end of the two-couple Texas-style Docey Do. The action survived as the four-couple Dos Paso.

Al Brundage remembered the details of that negotiation this way:

> At that time I was getting enthusiastic about the "western" style of dancing and the various new movements that were starting to be introduced into the activity. The DoPaso vs. DoceyDoe/Dosado/Dosido argument was a hot issue and I recall being a strong advocate of the back-to-back Dos a Dos as we had been doing it in New England. At the same time Shaw was trying to standardize certain movements and the question came up about touching hands on the Right & Left Through. I hung in for no-hands since that is what we were doing in New England and at the (Stepney) Barn - and it was the only way I had seen it done until I went to Shaw's. Shaw put these movements to a vote to try and get a "feel" for what the representatives from various sections of the U.S. wanted. I made a deal with Herb Greggerson that I would vote for the "use hands" Right & Left Through if he would let Dos a Dos alone and let it be Back-to-back. Then I would also vote for the term DoPaso if he accepted it - which, after heated discussions with Shaw, he did.

7

## WHAT MAKES "MODERN" SQUARE DANCING DIFFERENT?

Modern Western Square Dancing was born soon after the end of the war. It has become quite different from the traditional form of square dancing. From the perspective of fifty years later, it is possible to identify the changes that mark this difference. Foremost among them is a dance routine that changes as it is danced. The caller "creates" the patterns of modern square dances as they are called. The vocabulary of calls or dance actions is known to the dancers but the caller combines them into patterns that change with each sequence. Traditional square dancing experienced little change for more than a century. Although many books were published describing dance routines, the dances were more likely to be passed on orally. Callers attending other callers' dances would identify and "collect" material. These routines were often modified a bit with each new passing. Sometimes the routine was identified with a particular musical melody. Experienced dancers knew the steps of each dance and the caller or prompter reminded them if they weren't sure. The prompter also got the whole group started on each section of the dance at the same time. A caller's popularity was influenced by the rhymes and rhythms of his chanting delivery of the calls. That did not, however, make him easy to understand and success on the floor often depended on the dancers' knowledge of what came next.

Somewhere, someone decided that the set routine of a dance could be changed as people were dancing it. Perhaps it was because sound amplification equipment had improved enough by the war's end so that the dancers could actually understand the caller. Some callers were still shouting into megaphones. In some places each square had a caller and these callers didn't always call the same actions for their square that the other squares were doing. Even where there was public address equipment, it often was not adequate to assure that all the dancers on the floor could hear and understand what the caller was saying.

Equipment improvements made it possible to change the dance actions from those the dancers expected. The caller could be more than a prompter reminding dancers of memorized routines and could actually change the order in which the parts of the dance were done. This changing of the dance actions as they were executed is the most important distinction between what is called "western" or "modern" square dancing and its traditional form.

The name "western" suggests that the first steps along this new path were taken in the American West somewhere. It will probably not be possible to establish the exact place and time when this began. While we will probably never know what callers were involved with the first experiments with improvised choreography, there are some likely candidates. In his book *Cowboy Dances,* first published in 1939, Lloyd Shaw describes several "standard introductions." He goes on to say, "Any one of these can be substituted for any other according to the fancy of the caller." Ralph Page also says, in a syllabus he wrote for a California Folk Dance Camp in the late 1950's, "The charm of New England squares is not necessarily the complexity of figure, but the sudden interpolation of surprise calls which the competent caller inserts in the chorus figure, or anywhere at all for that matter." Later on the same page he says, "Also, New England callers are expert at taking a basic figure and improvising on the theme on the spur of the moment." My personal experience as a dancer was that the extent of variation in Ralph's routines was seldom more than exchanging a Right Allemande for a Left Allemande.

Although Ralph Page would not wish to be identified as a contributor to what he came to regard as a corruption of square dancing, the improvisation that he mentions is one of the fundamental differences between the traditional and modern forms of this activity. That improvisation came into the activity slowly. In the late 1940's the dance routines were passed from one caller to another either by word of mouth or by copying from a performance. Many of the routines had been passed from one generation to another. Some of the changes resulting from this "folk process" may have been the result of faulty memory while others may have been considered improvements.

A series of summer institutes organized by Lloyd Shaw in Colorado Springs, Colorado functioned as a school for callers. These were held before the war and started again in 1947. They continued each summer into the 1950's. Many of those who would become leaders in the development of modern square dancing attended one or more of these schools. These future leaders included Al Brundage and Ralph Page from New England, Herb Greggerson from El Paso, and Ralph Maxheimer from Southern California. Bob Osgood attended several of these training camps. He was also from Southern California and was the founding editor of *Sets in Order* magazine which became the most widely-read national square dance publication. At these meetings new ideas were discussed and styles of dancing from several regions of the country became known to all.

Shortly after Dr. Shaw started his schools, Herb Greggerson started schools for callers in Riodoso, New Mexico. Several callers attended both schools in the same summer. Undoubtedly the sharing of experience among those attending provided the earliest steps toward standardization. Herb was one of the earliest callers to travel the country. Al and his brother Bob Brundage recall attending a meeting with Herb held in southeastern Massachusetts in January 1950. Other leaders from the area who were present include Charlie Baldwin, then editor of the brand new magazine *The New England Caller,* and Howard Hogue who a couple of years later built Square Acres, a square dance center in East Bridgewater, Massachusetts. Bob remembers that Herb introduced the calls Dos Paso and Allemande Thar which were unknown in traditional New England square dancing.

## WHY DID THE CHANGE HAPPEN?

A new style of dancing in the first five years following WWII was defined and widely spread by Lloyd Shaw. Regional differences in square dance calls and execution became known through those same schools - both Shaw's and Greggerson's. Standardization began as callers who learned others' styles and techniques returned home and introduced what they had learned to their own dancers. This introduction process often took the form of classes and these, in turn, led to the formation of clubs. These sometimes small groups were economically possible because improved sound equipment allowed the use of recorded music. S. Foster Damon noted that, "...the second World War swept away our last romantic notions that Europeans were better than Americans; the nation worked together as never before; and again, as in 1651, the spirit of democracy rose from the folk into the ballrooms...The big recording companies began publishing albums of square-dances, to meet the new demand...one did not have to hire a caller and a band and a hall any more: one needed only ten feet square of floor-space, a phonograph, and four willing couples."

All of these contributed to the rapid growth of square dance popularity that began soon after the troops came home. None of them, however, answers the question of WHY the form of the dance changed. Was it because callers got bored and decided to experiment with changes to the choreography or was it because dancers somehow indicated an interest in change? I remember as a teenager dancing the common visiting-couple routines of the late 1940's. We discovered that when Couple One led out to Couple Two it was possible for Couple Three to do the same actions with Couple Four - without being told to do so by the caller. Did the callers notice these innovations by the dancers and respond to them by calling the action that way? Or had the callers already started to introduce these changes themselves? I doubt that anyone will ever provide a convincing answer to these questions, but the process was well underway by the start of the 1950's.

## THE SITUATION IN 1950

After WWII, the popularity of square dancing grew steadily. Most dances were held in public halls and organized by callers or orchestras. Square dance "clubs" were not widespread although in Southern California they were formed in great numbers during the late 1940's. One reason for this was the need to have real people to provide the music for dancing. While there were a few recordings of square dances available before 1950, they usually included a caller directing one of the standard dance routines of the day. Those that did not include calling were recorded at widely varying speed and could not be used on the usual record playing equipment available at the time.

Public address systems were becoming available and some included record players. A few of them allowed for changing the speed of rotation of the turntable so that the musical tempo (number of beats per minute) could be slowed or speeded up. Availability of this equipment was important to the growth of square dance clubs. With records it was possible to have music for square dancing without the expense of hiring live musicians. The only person needed was the caller.

In the early 1950's, square dance music recordings also became more available. The first companies to regularly produce square dance records with music only that were intended for a caller to use were C. P. Mac Gregor, and Folkcraft. C. P. MacGregor had been issuing records with Fenton "Jonesy" Jones and Les Gotcher calling in the late 1940's. When others who were involved in square dancing wanted to make square dance records Mr. Mac Gregor wasn't interested. One of those who got turned down was "Doc" Alambaugh who responded by starting Windsor Records in 1949. Several other square dance record labels were started during the early 1950's. Some of the major labels, notably Capital Record Company, also put out some records with music only.

The increasing availability of suitable recorded music made an important contribution to the growth of square dance clubs. Callers started teaching people to dance in a series of weekly lessons using recorded music. These early classes were often taught in someone's home. Graduates of the classes then started forming clubs so they could continue to enjoy their newly learned skills. The square dance club, a group of people who formed an organization for the primary purpose of sponsoring square dances, was one of the distinguishing characteristics of the modern form of square dancing. Nearly all traditional dancing was arranged by the caller or the orchestra. Traditional dancing was, and still is, done mostly with live musicians. Modern square dance groups rely heavily on recorded music to establish and maintain regular programs of dancing without the expense of an orchestra.

California was probably the first area to introduce change into the form and format of square dancing. Dr. Shaw was not trying to introduce change with his summer institutes but that may have been an unintended byproduct of those sessions. The formation of square dance clubs began in Southern California soon after WWII. Bob Osgood attended the first of the Postwar schools (1947) set up by Dr. Shaw in Colorado Springs. He reports that he and others realized that the style of dancing Dr. Shaw showed them could not be taught to dancers in a Saturday night, open-dance environment which was then the common format for square dancing nearly everywhere. They started teaching classes and this led to the formation of clubs.

Another factor was unique in the development of square dancing in Southern California. The movie industry included square dance scenes in several pictures. Early callers living in the area were hired to assist with these scenes. Les Gotcher writes about his experiences working in "twenty or more" movies in his book *Les Gotcher's Textbook of American Square Dancing,* published in 1961. Bob Osgood reports in the early issues of *Sets in Order* that he also consulted on several movies.

In New England, the earliest modern square dance clubs were all started in the 1950's. One of the first was the Connecticut Square Dance Club, started by Al Brundage after he returned from a tour of the Southwest in 1949. Al then started the Hartford (Connecticut) Square Dance Club. He was also instrumental in spreading the western style of dancing in other parts of New England. Al Monte, who was a teenage traditional caller in northern Vermont, learned about the "new" way of square dancing from Al during his visits to the area in the early 1950's. In East Bridgewater, Massachusetts Howard Hogue built a square dance hall in 1953 and several clubs formed to dance there. Howard also taught square dance classes in Newbury, Massachusetts where the Newbury Square Riggers were formed in the early 1950's. Howie Davidson came from "downeast" Maine to teach classes that became the Down East Western Square Dance Club in Kittery, Maine.

There were a few traditional square dance clubs in existence in the late 1940's. Sometimes they converted to the new way of dancing. One example is the Seacoast Region (of New Hampshire) Square Dance Club. The club was formed in 1949 dancing the traditional form with an orchestra and Mal Hayden calling for them once a month. Over the next decade they became a modern square dance group meeting weekly and sponsoring two classes each year to introduce new people to the activity. That club celebrated their 50th anniversary in September, 1999. This same pattern was followed by the Fitchburg (Massachusetts) Quadrille Club which started with a program of monthly traditional square dances with an orchestra. After conversion to modern square dancing the club changed its name to the Star Promenaders.

All along the east coast clubs were beginning to form. The formation process was usually the same. Either a traditional caller learned of changes that were taking place and gathered a small group to try the new ways or the dancers managing a traditional square dance group decided to shift to the new style of square dancing. One of those who was slow to make the transition to modern square dancing was Don Armstrong. He had a very successful traditional program in Florida and was not eager to experiment.

*Steps in Time,* a book published by the North Texas Square and Round Dance Association (NORTEX) in 1985, describes the formation of square dance clubs even before WWII. These clubs danced the local form of traditional square dancing with live musicians. The oldest club still in existence when the NORTEX book was published is the Circle Eight Square Dance Club that formed in 1947 dancing with live orchestras. The transition to the modern style probably took place in the next decade as additional clubs were formed throughout the 1950's.

One of the earliest of the traveling callers was Herb Greggerson. He had been calling since the mid-1930's and his demonstration group, The Blue Bonnet Set, put on their show at the 1939 World's Fair in New York. After his discharge from the U.S. Navy in 1946, he continued to travel as a full-time caller. He was one of those who attended Lloyd Shaw's 1947 school in Colorado Springs. Over the next five years he built a square dance hall in El Paso and offered a square dance institute for leaders in Riodoso, New Mexico.

In Quebec Province and the Canadian Maritimes, quadrilles were everywhere with the calls mostly given in French. The routines were similar to what was being danced in the northeastern U.S. Betty Peters, the wife of caller Bill Peters, grew up in the northwestern U.S. and remembers that square dances in her youth were called quadrilles. Development into the

13

modern style of square dance in western Canada followed the pattern set in California. An early caller who made a solid transition to the modern, club system was Earl Parke of Yorkton, Saskatchewan. He started in 1950 with a program for high school students sponsored by the Rotary Club. He reported to me that the students wanted to learn square dancing because Princess Elizabeth (now the Queen of England) had square danced during a visit to Ottawa. One of the longest running square dance programs anywhere was the annual summer festival in Penticton, British Colombia. Another was the Alberta Square Dance Institute that began in 1955 and was held annually in The Banff School of Fine Arts.

American square dancing was exported to countries outside North America by American servicemen and the U.S. State Department. Bob Osgood and Ralph Page were sent to Europe and Japan by the State Department to demonstrate and teach. Cal Golden was stationed in the U.S. Army in Germany and his job was managing Non-Commissioned Officer Clubs. He introduced and sustained the square dance programs there starting in the mid-1950's. A 1949 issue of *Sets in Order* magazine describes square dancing in Hokkaido, Japan, brought there by Winfield Niblo of Denver. The article mentions that the Emperor's brothers happened by and joined in the dancing.

# CHAPTER 2 - SQUARE DANCE POPULARITY EXPLODES

The decade of the '50's was a period of huge growth for square dancing. Two National publications were established. *Sets in Order* magazine began in 1949. It had a mid-life name change to *Square Dance* but nearly everyone referred to it as *Sets in Order* throughout its thirty-six year existence. *American Squares* was converted from a mimeographed newsletter to a printed periodical in 1947. (It went through a couple of name and ownership changes before being renamed *American SquareDance* by then owners Stan and Cathy Burdick in 1972.) *The New England Caller* magazine was first published in 1951 and its name also changed, in July 1987, to *The Northeast Square Dancer Magazine*. Many other regional periodicals began publication at about that time. Throughout the decade new clubs were started in nearly every part of the U.S. and Canada and in many overseas locations as well. In Chapter 4 we will look more closely at the pace of growth that began in the early 1950's.

Formation of new clubs was often initiated by dancers who wanted a club closer to their home. They then either found a caller willing to call for the new group or encouraged someone from their dancer group to learn to call. My own experience is typical. I returned to the city where I grew up after being discharged from the Army. In 1954, at a traditional square dance, a couple in my square spoke up in the middle of the evening. They had recognized that I was familiar with the modern style of dancing. Vi and Wendell Parker, had been introduced to this new way of square dancing in Barre, Vermont where Wendell managed the local Newbury's Five & Dime store. Transferring to Manchester, New Hampshire and learning that I was a caller he asked if I would call for a group of friends in the basement of their home. Within six months, the newly formed Allemande 8's Square Dance Club sponsored their first class in the Manchester YMCA. That first class was about six squares recruited fairly easily by the eight couples that had been dancing in the Parkers' basement.

By 1957, the club included a few members from Nashua, a city eighteen miles to the south. Nashua residents wanted to have a club of their own and encouraged me to offer a class to get it started. Recruitment of that class is of particular interest in the current recruiting environment. As a longtime resident of Nashua, I was able to persuade the church couples' clubs in town to give me the names and addresses of their members. I wrote letters to two hundred couples (and this was before the days of computer-prepared direct mailing). I also knew that a letter by itself wouldn't do the job, so the week before the first class I called most of those two hundred couples. Many assured me that they found it interesting and that they would plan to be there but not one of those couples showed up. In fact, only one non-dancing couple came that first night. The one couple that did show up was encouraged to come back with some of their friends. After several weeks of encouraging those who did come to return with more of their friends, we were able to start a class that was at least large enough to pay for the cost of the hall. That group became the Border City Squares club which recently celebrated its forty-five year anniversary.

Another window through which we can view the state of square dancing in the 1950's comes to me in a communication from Cal Campbell who is still active as a caller at the turn of the century. He is describing square dancing at Colorado A & M in Fort Collins, Colorado.

Many of the local clubs had multiple callers. Each caller brought his own records and signed up for the dance they wanted to call. Someone would mark the selections on a black board and people watched to see if they knew each dance.

The college square dance club was called the Aggie Haylofters. You attended a series of 10 weekly lessons which provided enough experience and knowledge that you could dance anyplace. The Haylofters club was the second largest student organization on campus and definitely the place to meet girls.

I started learning to become a caller in the fall of 1955. I picked up one record for patter and picked a dance from *Sets in Order Five*

*Years Of Dancing* and memorized it. I also did the same with a singing call. This was the accepted method of learning to call and you didn't stray very far from the routines published in the books.

In 1955 the change from calling named routines to calling "hash"[2] was just starting on the eastern slope of the Rockies. We attended some dances where the program was not set and you had to just get on the floor and listen to the caller. When the caller had something different, he would walk the pattern. Every dance tip was built around a theme.

There was only one caller in Ft. Collins that was considered a club caller. He and his wife had built a dance hall and sold what they called square dance clothes. He used a mixture of "hash" and fixed routines. He seldom notified you of what was coming up on the program. He just called.

Traveling callers were usually only employed for special dances. The Aggie Haylofters held a big annual weekend of dances in the spring of each year and I can remember meeting some of the people who later became my idols. However, they were a novelty and not the mainstay of the square dance movement in Colorado.

I have received communications from several callers who were active in the 1950's. One of these, Richard Wilson, tells of the situation in the Phoenix, Arizona area and reflects the earlier establishment of square dance clubs in that region.

I called square dances in the 1950's in Arizona, mostly in Phoenix. There were several clubs that belonged to the Valley of The Sun Square Dance Association. Most of the clubs had a live band. They had a different caller for each tip.

We had a callers association where we met and shared information. Dancers were invited and you could try new material. We each had a list, somewhat alike. I called hash and also put various patterns to various songs. Most of the callers only did singing calls.

---

2 "Hash" was a term that came into use during the 1950's. It referred to the mixing of dance routines that distinguished modern square dancing from traditional.

Sources of our material came from *Set's in Order* and a magazine by Les Gotcher. [It is interesting to note that the "magazine" is probably the *Notes for Callers* published by Les the first issue of which came out in April 1960.] The record company was Old Timer Records and Western Jubilee. I don't remember too many of the callers [but two were] Mike Michelle and Johnny Shultz. Mike had a barn on Indian School Road. We danced at the Western Saddle Club during the summer.

I usually called every Friday, Saturday and Sunday also taught a class. The winter resorts would have you call a dance. Most of the clubs were associated with the schools.

Another caller, Stew Shackllette, wrote that in the late 1940's around Louisville, Kentucky "...we danced mostly visiting couple dances...There were a few singing calls like Hot Time in the Old Town Tonight, Spanish Cavellero and Red Wing with the dip and dive across the square." Stew moved to California in 1951 and it was there that he first encountered the western type of dance material. He wrote that, "We were starting to use both Head Couples leading to the right, which involved all the dancers, and two couples did not have to stand and wait for their turn." He returned to Kentucky in 1955 and soon after "started a square dance class which had 27 squares. Of course the lessons were only 16 weeks at that time. By this time we were using Square thru and a host of Allemande variations." The only traveling caller that he can remember coming through Louisville was Ed Gilmore.

New England was, in fact, among the slowest regions to start the formation of modern square dance groups. While the process was well underway in the Southwest, and in Southern California by 1950, that was the time of the formation of the first clubs in New England. Al Brundage had toured the Southwest in 1949 and reported on the experience in the September 1951 issue of *The New England Caller* magazine as follows:

Many of you folks have noticed the change in my terminology from Docey-doe to DoPaso. Why this sudden change? Well, about two years ago I toured throughout the Southwest and was very much impressed with the quality of the dancing and the huge number of enthusiastic participants. I found this was due to two things.

First, an organized program of square-dance classes where complete knowledge of basic fundamentals was taught so that people learned to dance properly.  These people eventually organized or joined in square-dance clubs where they continued their dancing fun with other couples like themselves.

Second, the figures danced by these folks were of the intermediate and advanced level and were built around a basic movement known as the Docey-doe.  This was very intriguing.  Here was something smooth and danceable that eliminated the "swing" with all its dizzying effects and forearms—a lifesaver for middle-aged and older couples who soon tired of dancing "swing games" all night.

Well, I figured if I took these two facts and inaugurated them into the square dance picture here at home I could overcome much of what seemed to be ailing our dances and our dancers.  Thus, I organized classes, encouraged clubs, and started teaching and building calls around the docey-doe.

Now, folks here in New England have always done a do-si-do (dos-a-dos) which is the "back to back" movement.  The introduction of the "new" Docey-doe with its "partner left - corner right" action sent shivers through many staunch Yankees.  Many of them refused to join the groups and classes and labeled this strange maneuver as "Western" and refused to have any part of it.  Besides, who was I to teach innocent citizens that Docey-doe meant this hand business when everyone knew that Dos-a-dos (pronounced do-si-do) meant back to back?

Well, it seems that other leaders throughout New England were having the same trouble and the loss of sleep due to this issue was making many people hard to get along with.  So, we all got together and figured the only practical solution for us here in New England was to adopt the term coined by Pappy Shaw and now used widely in many sections of the country - DoPaso.  So, when your caller breaks you into a DoPaso, turn your partner with your left hand and your corner with your right hand - hands and arms in an upright position (with elbow bent) so that you can get a good firm grip and swing each other around with this one hand.

Yours for relaxin' dancing, Al Brundage

The paragraph in the middle of that article beginning "Well, I figured…" probably describes what started the change from the traditional to the modern form of square dancing in New England. Al's trip was in 1949. Conversations with Bob Osgood suggest that a very similar process took place in Southern California a couple of years earlier. Bob reports that the visits by the Lloyd Shaw, Cheyenne Mountain Dancer demonstration group generated interest in the kind of dancing they were doing. This type of dancing was smoother and more intricate than the traditional square dancing which was common in the area at that time. Bob was motivated to attend the Shaw summer institutes in Colorado Springs and came home wanting to promote the type of dancing that Shaw was teaching.

The modern style of square dancing spread from the Southwest to the rest of the U.S. and Canada. One of the major means for spreading the word was the demonstrations of the Cheyenne Mountain Dancers. They traveled widely during the school's summer vacations. Local callers were often recruited to attend the Shaw Square Dance Institutes in Colorado Springs. Another important factor in the spread of the new style was the traveling callers. One of the earliest and most active was Herb Greggerson. For a few years in the late 1940's, Herb was the most traveled of the callers. Soon after he started his own square dance institutes in Riodoso, New Mexico, he curtailed his traveling. There were, however, many others to take his place on the road.

Foremost among the traveling emissaries were Ed Gilmore and Les Gotcher. Both covered the U.S. and Canada almost continuously throughout the decade of the '50's. They were quite different in both heritage and approach. Les had been calling before the War. He presented a cowboy image in both dress and the inflection of his voice. He looked a bit like the movie star Gregory Peck and, in fact, was involved in a few movies as a square dance caller and/or consultant.[3] His style of calling was a driving, rhythmic chant. He was, by his own admission, not a singer and rarely used a singing call in his dance program. Ed Gilmore, by contrast, had started calling in 1947. He was, at the time, the owner of a hardware store. His calling popularity and the growth of interest in square dancing quickly turned him into a full-time caller. In 1949 he was teaching a class for callers and was in demand for the staffing of festivals distant from his Yucaipa, California home. His calling style was relaxed and emphasized the music far more than Les's. Ed decided early that a sense of dancing was important

---

[3] Quite a number of movies have included square dance segments. Among these are: "Duel In the Sun", "Square Dance Jubilee" and "Copper Canyon". Les was not the only caller involved in these productions. Bob Osgood served as a consultant on "Giant" and "Pardners" which starred Jerry Lewis and Dean Martin.

while the emphasis in Les's calling was on the intricacy of the dancing action.

Together, Ed and Les had a huge influence on the spread of modern square dancing. I remember that, after a Les Gotcher tour through New England, nearly every caller developed a bit of a "western" twang - which seemed particularly strange in some who usually spoke with a strong "downeast" accent. Les also started every tip with "Walk All Around the Left Hand Lady, See Saw Your Pretty Little Taw" and for weeks after his tours so did most of the New England callers. Ed Gilmore was particularly interested in teaching callers. It was common for local associations of callers to contract with Ed for a day or weekend clinic. His influence on the developing skills and philosophy of new callers was widespread. For many years he ran an annual school for callers in Glenwood Springs, Colorado.

The profit potential of the calling tour grew steadily through the 1950's. New square dance clubs were forming everywhere. There was a mystique surrounding the caller from somewhere else - anywhere else. Most of the early traveling callers were from California. A few came out of Texas. In New England, at this time, only a couple of callers were known outside the immediate vicinity of New England. Ralph Page was widely recognized as a dean of traditional square dancing and contra dancing. He was sent by the U.S. State Department to many foreign lands as a cultural ambassador. He was not, however, at all interested in the "new" form of square dancing. The other New England caller who was known - and hired - outside the region was Al Brundage. He had been hired for festivals in the Southwest and in Chicago in the late '40's and he continued as a regular on the festival circuit. Al's home program that grew to include several clubs for whom he called regularly and taught classes, kept him from taking to the road for any extended trips.

During the 1950's many of the traveling callers who came through New England from California were associated in some way with Bob Osgood and the *Sets in Order* magazine. Among these were Arnie Kronenberger, Bruce Johnson, Lee Helsel and Bob Page. Callers who were not, particularly, associated with *Sets in Order* also traveled the country regularly. Among those who visited New England were Marshall Flippo from Texas, Max Forsyth from Indiana and Bill Castner from the San Francisco area. Gilmore and Gotcher also came to New England but they were the only ones then traveling full-time. Many early traveling callers were school teachers and they toured most extensively in the summer.

There was a substantial overlap between callers who traveled and those who called at major square dance festivals. Early in the 1950's there were several well-established regional festivals that hired the traveling callers as staff. These festivals or conventions used local area callers for some of the program and featured the travelers in the evening program. In 1949 radio station WLS (The Prairie Farmer Station) in Chicago sponsored the first in a continuing series of festivals. The staff was Ed Gilmore (who, it should be noted, had been calling only two years at that time), Al Brundage and Dr. Ralph Piper. Dr. Piper was a professor at the University of Minnesota teaching physical education and was one of the earliest leaders in the growth of square dancing in the midwestern U.S. Although he was one of the founders of this event, by the third WLS International Festival in 1952, he had been replaced on the staff by Herb Greggerson.

Popularity undoubtedly bred more popularity. Callers that dancers heard at the festivals to which they traveled were the ones they hired as "visiting" callers for their clubs. Callers also hired each other as they started running weekend dance institutes or week-long dance vacation programs. Al Brundage was one of the earliest callers to recognize the business potential of caller-run events for the dancers. Perhaps they followed the model established by Dr. Shaw whose summer institutes were not, exclusively, for callers. Herb Greggerson started a school in Riodoso, NM. Ralph Page offered a week-long summer dance program in Peterborough, New Hampshire and it was there that I first tried calling in the summer of 1949. The first issue of *The New England Caller Magazine*, published in August 1951, mentions that about seventy-five teachers, callers and dancers attended Al Brundage's 2nd Summer Square Dance School that year. The curriculum at these schools included mostly dance routines and styling. The process of learning to call in those days was strongly focused on developing a set of memorized dance routines. A school for dancers that taught dance routines was also useful for those learning to call.

During the 1950's and 1960's Al ran many week-long and weekend square dance events with staff callers from outside New England. These events introduced his staff callers to the leaders of clubs who then hired them to call for their clubs - often on the same trips that brought them to Brundage-run events. New England became very popular with traveling callers.

Al describes planning his first square dance "week" at the Hotel Green in Danbury, Connecticut:

Back home in Connecticut not many dancers understood what was going on in those days and most of them had never seen some of the Western movements. They were perfectly happy doing what they were doing and saw no need to add or change anything...So I thought if I could get some real western person with a good sense of music - timing & phrasing to come in and be the "Nationally Known 'expert'" from Texas & California that he might be able to "sell" the idea of more movements and new styling. Then I would be able to carry it on after he left town. This is about what happened and I made a great choice of leaders when I chose Ed Gilmore. I had considered others such as Ralph Maxheimer, Manning Smith (who was into calling rather than Rounds in those days) Herb Greggerson, Jim York, Carl Journel and a few others who were also at Shaw's and seemed to be strong leaders. I was just the "young kid on the block" at that time and I had to borrow money to put a deposit down on the Hotel Green. I was running scared for quite some time until the applications started coming and it was obvious that I would be able to pay the expenses and run a successful weekend...From that first weekend I went on to bring in others and I was able to get them bookings throughout New England in order to make the trip more inviting for them to come.

The callers brought into the area by Al were some of the most popular traveling callers of the 1950's and 1960's. Included were Bruce Johnson, Johnny LeClair, Max Forsyth, Marshall Flippo, Dave Taylor, Ken Bower, Jerry Haag and Gary Shoemake.

## THE EARLY STAGES OF DIVISION

The modern form of square dancing has always included in its identification the word "western." It is not exactly clear where that terminology originated, but in the early 1950's there were significant differences between the way square dancing was done in New England and the way it was done "out west." Howard "Hogie" Hogue was a dancer in the west before coming to New England. He reports on his trip to Shaw's School in the October 1951 issue of *The New England Caller*.

I was very interested to get West and see just what had happened to square dancing in the last ten years. Wow! What a change from the old visiting couple dances, with the caller far from any idea of timing, rhythm, or music, to dances like "Throw in The Clutch," "Yucaipa Twister," etc., and the callers phrasing perfectly, with good rhythm, and slowed down from 160 to 140 (beats per minute)—which is still pretty fast.

Now, East versus West. You have probably already said 'Hogie is a great one to make that his comparison,' but I like to feel that I am broad-minded enough to see a clear picture. I made this statement in the West: New England has its feet more firmly on the ground than any other part of the country as I have the picture. Square dancing here is better controlled by people with a genuine interest in this form of dancing thus giving a more healthy outlook for the future of square dancing in the East. It has not ballooned out of proportion as it has in California where, for instance, you might refer to "the guy who has a tiger by the tail." The West is on top as far as dancing and calling are concerned. Singing calls are being used very sparingly but nevertheless are coming in. The entire country without question is feeling the powerful influence of Mr. Shaw. Whether you agree or not, Pappy HAS more influence over the whole picture than any other ten men so all I can say is that we're fortunate it is a man of his caliber who is at the top.

In 1952 Al Brundage writes, again in *The New England Caller*, about his trip west:

We had lots of fun with the California people. They have a great love for dancing and a tremendous spirit. This shows through at their dances and it is a treat to dance with them as they are excellent dancers - well grounded - and they enjoy themselves thoroughly. My job was to introduce Contras. Many Californians are only lukewarm on contras and this because most of them have no sense of phrasing, combined with the fact that they shortcut many of their steps. They seem to be in a hurry to get somewhere else. This seems to be a little silly to me and of course doesn't work out too well in dancing contras.

These two observations indicate an early recognition of some difference between the way the East, or at least, New England, was dancing and the way folks danced in other areas. In fact Ricky Holden wrote about the differences in part in a book entitled *The Square Dance Caller,* published in 1951. (The phrasing that he mentions is the phrase of the music which is usually made up of four 16-beat melodic phrases for a total of 64 beats before the song starts over again.)

Eastern square dancing is very often phrased completely with the music, 1 - 64, and it is always phrased 1-16. Eastern callers understand phrasing so well that it has become almost subconscious in their calling...

Western square dancing can be phrased 1 - 16, although this is not always possible or necessary, but it should always be phrased 1 - 4. Unfortunately a great many Western callers fail to phrase calls at all with the music, so the modern Western square dance development has grown up to ignore phrasing. Thus, many Western callers and more dancers have not had the chance to discover the advantage of dancing with the phrase of the music instead of just the beat.

Southern Mountain square dancing can be phrased 1 - 4. However so much of the Mountain style involves individual footwork that it is generally up to each dancer to phrase his stepping while the caller merely suggests the next figure in a loud voice.

In the first decade of "modern" square dancing it was often called western with the clear implication that non-western dancing was done in the East. Looking back, it is easy to see that the "new" form of square dancing was born in the West and, even more specifically, the Southwest and California. It spread slowly to other regions and was identified as western square dancing to differentiate it from whatever the local form of square dancing may have been. It would be easy to assume that this new style of dancing completely replaced the old fashioned kind in the West. This is certainly not true. Traditional square dancing continued there as it did in most areas. There is no question that traditional square dancing did survive, and sometimes thrive, in some areas, even as the popularity of the modern style grew rapidly.

# CHAPTER 3 - CHOREOGRAPHY IN THE 1950'S

Clearly an important difference between traditional and modern square dancing as we start a new millennium, is the vocabulary of calls. As the decade of the 1950's began, there was a set of ten to twenty calls in use. They were common to both the traditional and modern forms of square dancing. The distinction that was beginning to grow between traditional and modern square dancing was based on the way the calls were used as well as on the calls themselves.

## CALL VOCABULARY

We have several ways of identifying the calls in use at that time. An article in a 1950 issue of *Sets in Order* gives a list of "calls done in Texas" as listed by Ricky Holden, a wide-roaming caller, to accompany a record he had made. The listed calls were:

Allemande, Grand Right &Left, Ladies Chain, Right & Left Thru,
Do Si Do, Sashay (or All Around) and Catch All Eight.

All of these, except Catch All Eight, are the most standard of traditional calls. In his notes for a caller school in 1949, Ed Gilmore lists the calls that should be taught as:

Allemande Left, Grand Right and Left, Promenade, Swing, Dos-A-Dos, Docey-doe, Do Paso, Right and Left Thru, Ladies Chain and See Saw, Star, All Around (Left Hand Lady), California Twirl and Circle.

A number of books were published in the late 1940's that listed the calls then in use. We can compare these to give us insight into calls that were widely used and those that were more local. We may also compare documents of a clearly traditional dance environment such as *Good Morning* published by Henry Ford in 1943 and the book *Honor Your Partner* by Ed Durlacher in 1949 as well as books that represented or were the work of callers headed for the modern form. These comparisons confirm that those we have listed were the common call vocabulary of 1950.

CALLERLAB, the International Association of Square Dance Callers, an organization formed in 1974, publishes a list of calls that has become a worldwide standard. In it twenty calls are identified as traditional in origin. To the calls named previously, the CALLERLAB list adds: Forward & Back, Pass Thru, Split the Outside Couple, Separate, Lead Right, Grand Square, Circle to a Line and Dive Thru. This listing raises a couple of questions. My review of a wide variety of resources of the pre-1950 period shows only one mention of Grand Square. That is in Henry Ford's *Good Morning*. This book is also the only one in which I find mention of Pass Through and it is not the action we now intend with that call. The one mention is in the singing call "The Girl I Left Behind Me." The instruction is:

> The head couple lead up to the right and balance there so kindly
>> And pass right through and balance, too
> and swing that girl behind you

Its meaning there appears to be more of a simple, common-language direction than a call that dancers would be expected to learn. Another question raised by this search of early call lists concerns the call Circle to a Line. Again, the only mention of it I have found before 1950 is in *Good Morning*. There it is listed under the heading "Miscellaneous Calls" in a dance called "Eight in Line." The direction is:

> Head couples lead to right, circle four hands around, and stop (four in line)

> (Two lines are now standing opposite and facing each other.)

No information or explanation of how to convert the circle of four to the facing lines is included.

Whatever other calls may have existed, it is clear that the set of calls in common use in 1950 is quite short. Nearly all are still in use in both modern and traditional square dancing today. There are a number of other calls that were in use in some areas and there are also extensions of the listed calls. Ladies Chain, for instance, is done by both two and four ladies. Ricky Holden's Sashay was more commonly called Walk All Around the Left Hand Lady and it was nearly always followed by See Saw Your Taw. Ed Gilmore used Dos a Dos Corner in place of the Walk Around. Do Si Do is a separate issue entirely. The Eastern form of this was Dos a Dos and derived from the French language words meaning Back to Back. Docey Do was a Western form and was considerably more complex. The similarity of name for actions so very different was probably the reason that Dr. Shaw negotiated the compromise action Dos Paso which in form was close to the Docey Do but in name was easily distinguished from the Dos a Dos.

Modern square dancers find it difficult to imagine that entire evenings of square dancing could be held using such a limited set of calls. One reason this was possible is that the dances involved many actions that were taught and described but were not calls that could be included in a list. Many examples can be found in any compilation of dances of the 1950's. They were written out in complete detail including not only the calls and other descriptions of action, but also the patter phrases that were to be used along with the calls.

As an example, consider the following dance from Ed Gilmore's 1949 class notes:

### INSIDE ARCH OUTSIDE UNDER

1. Introduction
2. Figure
   a. First couple out to the couple on the right, circle four hands half way around
   b. Inside arch and the outside under (repeat 3 more times)
   c. On to the next and circle half and don't you blunder.
   d. Inside arch and outside under
3. On to the next (Repeated)
   f. Balance home and everybody swing.
3. Chorus Call
   2nd, 3rd, and 4th couples repeat figure.

These directions use the words "Inside arch and the outside under" to describe an action used in this particular dance routine. Notice that the dance is named for this action which was not done in other dances. These actions were not considered "calls" that the dancers added to their regular vocabulary. They were learned actions that were part of this particular dance.

Here is another example from Ed Gilmore's notes that illustrates this distinction between "calls" and descriptive action.

### FOUR IN LINE YOU TRAVEL

1. Introduction
2. Figure
    a. First couple lead to the couple on the right and four in line you travel.
    b. Now I'll swing your girl you swing mine
    c. You swing that one while I'm gone and I'll take yours and travel on.
    d. Four in line you travel.
    e. Now I'll swing your girl you swing mine.
    f. You swing that one while I'm gone and I'll take yours and travel on.
    g. Four in line you travel
    h. I'll swing your girl you swing mine
    I. You swing that one while I'm gone and I'll take yours and travel on.

Everybody swing.

3. Chorus Call

Repeat three times until they have their own partners back then call an ending.

### EXPLANATION:

(a) First couple leads to the right side of couple #2 and standing in a line of four the two ladies hook right elbows and both couples walk forward or clockwise turning as a line of four until #1 gent returns to the center of the set.

(b) Gents release the ladies and turn to face their opposite as the ladies continue to turn until lady #2 is in the center of the set and the first gent swings the second lady as the second gent swings the first lady.

(c) The first gent takes the second lady on to couple #3 and they repeat (a & b).

(d) First gent takes third lady on to couple #4 and they repeat (a & b)

(e) First gent takes fourth lady back to his home position and all four couples swing.

These notes are for callers. Their purpose is to teach callers how to teach dances. Ed writes out the words for callers to use - and these include the words "Four in line you travel" which he does not include in his list of calls that must be taught. Clearly, dancers must be taught how to execute this dance action whether or not they know the calls that appear on Ed's list. The "EXPLANATION" contains the information that dancers must know in addition to the meaning of the calls.

The Gilmore notes start each dance with "Introduction" and end each with "Chorus Call." This indicates his intention that the choice of which introduction and chorus to use was optional. In his notes he includes a substantial section of introductions. A sampling of these is included here:

Honor your partner and the lady by your side
All join hands and circle wide
Break and swing with the pretty little thing
Promenade you promenade home.

Two, four, six, eight all join hands
Circle to the left as pretty as you can
The other way back on the same old track
Make those feet go whickety whack
Swing, Swing. Everybody swings.

Honor your partner and comers all
Circle left and don't you fall
Circles to the left go all the way 'round
With the big foot up and the little foot down
Hurry back home and swing 'em round

All jump up and never come down
Your honeys in your arms go round and round
Till the hollow of your foot makes a hole in the ground
And promenade, go promenade

The Gilmore notes also list a number of "Breaks." That is another term for "Chorus Call." Some examples:

## RIGHT AND LEFT GRAND

Allemande left with your left hand
Right to your partner right and left grand

## BACKTRACK

Allemande left like a hinge on a gate
Right to your parred and right and left eight
Corns in the crib, wheats in the sack
Meet your honey and turn a right back
Up the river and around the bend
The other way back you're gone again
Now your right you can't go wrong
Take her this time and promenade along

## ALLEMANDE THAR

Allemande left with an allemande thar
A right and left and form a star
Make that star to the heavens whirl
A right and left to the second girl
Allemande thar and form a star
Shoot that star and find your own
Turn her under your arm and promenade home

## TRIPLE ALLEMANDE

Allemande left and the ladies star
The gents run around but not too far
Allemande left and the gents star
The ladies run around but not too far
Allemande left with your left hand
Right to your pard and a right and left grand

Notice that the wording includes all the patter as well as the words needed to direct the dance action. The patter is intended to make each line take four beats of music. Ed expected that callers would memorize the full wording of the complete routine. There was no thought that such routines would be changed as they were called. It's also interesting to observe that, even as I write this nearly fifty years later, the words used to direct an Allemande Thar to modern dancers are often identical to those presented here. The Triple Allemande was also called in exactly this way until it disappeared from the common vocabulary somewhere in the 1970's.

This form of choreography was the starting point. In 1950 there was no recognized difference between modern and traditional square dancing. There was beginning to be a distinction between Western and Eastern square dancing. Those terms were used as we have seen in earlier chapters, however, they referred less to the vocabulary of calls than to the style of dancing. Square dancing in the East was thought to be less rowdy than in the West. Dance actions tended to fit the phrase of the music more in the East than in the West.

Comparison of calls listed in the various sources does suggest that addition of new calls to the vocabulary was going to mark the difference between these two styles of square dancing. A Western Docey Doe was never seen in the East. Dos Paso was really an invented call created by Dr. Shaw as described in an earlier chapter. Those calls that are included in most of the sources reviewed remain, fifty years later, as the core calls of traditional square dancing. There have been few additions. In the modern form of square dancing, however, the trickle of new calls that began about 1950 became a flood of hardly imaginable proportions within a couple of decades.

## NEW DANCE ROUTINES OR NEW CALLS?

The development of the square dance vocabulary during the 1950's is fairly easy to trace. In 1954, *Sets in Order* magazine published a book *5 Years of Square Dancing* that was a compilation of many of the routines that had appeared in the magazine during that period. Terms that later became the calls taught to nearly all dancers in class appeared first as complete dance routines. Two of these, Allemande Thar and Triple Allemande, are mentioned above as they appeared in Ed Gilmore's caller class notes. In the 5-Year book the actions that were not commonly known by dancers like Wagon Wheel, Alamo Style and Red Hot, were printed with explanations. Some terms that would become part of the dancers' standard vocabulary were described in detail when they appeared in print during this period. Terms like Box the Gnat, Wheel Around and Pass Thru are part of the most basic vocabulary today but needed separate explanation when they were first introduced. Pass Through is of particular interest because, as the spelling indicates, it was not thought of by most people as a call. In the 5-Year book it appears first in a routine called "Split the Ring and Around Just One," described below. This routine is a forerunner of a pattern that would become the foundation for a substantial part of the new way of square dancing. It came to be known as the "goal post" routine. Because it became such a central part of the next two decades of square dancing it is instructive to see how it was presented in this early publication.

**First four forward up and back**
Couples one and three

**Forward again and pass right through**
passing right shoulders with opposite head couples pass through but do not touch partner and do *not* turn her in place

**Split the ring and around just one**
Active couples split from their partners, women going right and men to left, meeting their opposite lady behind couple two and four.

**Down the center we'll have a little fun**
**Pass right through**
Man number one with lady number three go in between couple number four, while man three and lady one go together through couple two. They meet in the center and pass on through.

**Split the ring and around just one**
Go between couples two and four.
**Down the center and pass right through**
Active gents meet own partners and pass through other active couple.
**On the corner with your left hand**
Just the Texas way of saying Allemande Left.
**Right to your partner and right on by**
As you do in a right and left grand
**Left to the next and hold on tight**
**swing her around if it takes all night.**
After Passing partner with right hand each gent does a left "once-and-a-half" with his right hand girl, or the next one in line. The man then stands there with this new partner in *her* place.
**Same old gent and a brand new dame**
**Forward up and back again, etc...**

Man one with lady two and man three with lady four go through action again (repeat until men return home with original partner, then do four times for the sides.)

Another complete dance routine that would become a foundation pattern for modern square dancing also appeared in the 5-Year book. Its title is "The Route" and it is listed as "Origin Unknown." In it the action called "Open Up Into a Line" is described in some detail.

**First and Third Bow and Swing**
**Promenade Half Around the Ring**
No. 1 and No. 3 promenade around the outside, just changing places.
**Right and Left Thru Across the Set**
**Turn Right Back - You're Not Thru Yet**
No. 1 and No. 3 R. And L. Thru back to home position
**Two Ladies Chain Across the Way**
**Chain 'em Back - Don't Let 'em Stay**
No. 1 and No. 3. Ladies chain over and back.
**Same Two Couples Out to the Right and**
**Circle four - You're Doing Fine**
**Now Open Up Into a Line**
No. 1 goes to No.2 and No. 3 to No. 4 and circle almost once around and then No.1 and No. 3 gents let go of their corner ladies' hands opening into two lines of four facing one another. No. 1 and No. 3 should be at the end of the line closest to their home position. Lines are on No. 2 and No. 4 sides of square.
**Forward Eight and Back You Go**
**Forward Again for a Do-Sa-Do**
Two lines go forward and back, then forward again for a do-sa-do with opposite person.
**Now Right and Left Thru Across the Set**
**Then Right and Left Back - You're Not Thru Yet**
No 1 and No. 4 right and left thru and No. 2 and No 3 do same. Then back.
**With a Ladies Chain Across You Go**
Two ladies chain across the set - No. 1 with No. 4 and No. 2 with No. 3
**Chain Along the Line and Don't Be Slow**
The two ladies chain along each line. No. 1 lady, who is now with the No. 4 man, chains with No.2 lady, who is with No.3

man, and No. 3 lady, who is with No. 2 man, chains with No. 4
lady, who is No. 1 man.

**Across the Set You Chain Once More**

Two ladies chain across the set - No. 1 with No. 2 and No. 3
with No. 4

**Chain the Line as You Did Before**

Chain along the lines of four. No.1 with No. 2 and No. 3 with
No. 4

**Swing on the Corner and Little Bit Hard**

Swing corner girl.

**Now Swing Your Own in Your Own Back Yard**
**Allemande Left, etc.**

Repeat for couple No. 2 and No. 4.

These two examples - the "goal post" pattern and "the route" - were a
departure from the traditional forms of square dancing. They quickly
progressed from the set routines that were first presented in print. In the
early 1950's some callers started to change dance routines *as they called
them*. It was this change that was probably the first and most important
distinction between the traditional form of square dancing and what would
eventually become known as Modern Western Square Dancing.

In this chapter we have started to explore the changes in dance
choreography that marked the difference between the traditional and modern
forms of square dancing. There were substantial changes in both the
terminology - the actual call names - and in the way the dance patterns were
put together using these words. There were no more than twenty calls in
regular use in the early 1950's and the dance patterns were completely
memorized with variations introduced only "off mike." By the end of the
decade the vocabulary in regular use had more than doubled and both the
structure of the dance routine and the frequency of changes were
dramatically different. In Chapter 6, we will explore in considerably more
detail the specific differences in the structure of the dance.

# CHAPTER 4 - THE GROWTH OF CLUBS AND FESTIVALS

By the early 1950's the growth pattern for the new form of square dancing was well established. Callers and dancer leaders who had attended the Shaw's institutes in Colorado Springs and Herb Greggerson's institutes in Riudoso, New Mexico, went home and started square dance clubs. These clubs were different from the "open" public square dances that were usual in the traditional form of square dancing. Open, public dances were run by callers or by organizations as part of a general recreational program. The square dance club was an organization that existed primarily to provide a regular, usually weekly, program of square dancing. Clubs also sponsored square dance classes. Club members were active recruiters and contributed to an explosion of interest in square dancing.

This was a period of uneasiness in American society. There is a theory of social behavior which holds that, following wars, there is a need for people to return to their heritage and express it strongly. Square dancing fit this purpose beautifully. It was promoted as - and was - an expression of an uniquely American form of dance. It was also an excellent way to meet people and make friends. The square dance club was a strongly social organization. As a recreation for couples it was also unique. There were few group activities available that a couple could do together. Most sports like bowling and tennis were done in single-sex groups. This was an era when most women stayed home with the children while their men went off to work. A chance to get out of the house for an evening of recreation together was appealing to women. They brought their men to square dance class - often kicking and screaming in resistance.

Most of the couples that came to square dance classes were recruited by their friends. Men came on the first night reluctantly but then came back willingly. They found on the first night that square dancing was something they could do. It didn't take any fancy footwork. It did use their mind as well as their feet. It did distract them from whatever problems they had during the day and it was fun. In fact, it was often the men that kept the couple coming back to class although that wasn't a major task because the women were happy to get a night out with their partner away from the kids. This was also an era when other family members often lived nearby and could provide baby-sitting services. There is no question that the situation in American society made recruiting for square dance classes much easier in the 1950's than it is today.

The magnitude and the pace of the square dance popularity explosion are difficult to trace with great accuracy. Until the 1980's, there had never been any kind of census of square dancers and there is considerable question about the accuracy and validity of the attempt made then by an organization named Legacy. There are, however, a number of indicators that suggest a very strong growth in square dance participation during the 1950's and 1960's. We can note the formation of dancer organizations and caller organizations. We can also discover a growing number of festivals and conventions. Even as the modern form of it began to be different, square dancing was a thriving, successful recreation in many parts of the country. A few excerpts from the first year of *Sets in Order* magazine which began publication in November 1948 give us a sense of an already popular activity.

In the very first issue, a directory of dances listed twenty-eight square dance events in Southern California on Saturday nights. There were also listings of events on each of the weekdays. The February 1949 issue mentions "almost 200 Square Dance groups in the Los Angeles area." The April issue that year notes that "Between 1400 & 1600 dancers, members of the Associated Square Dancers, filled the Pan Pacific Auditorium on Sunday, February 27. Eleven callers, a recording orchestra and television were on hand." The May issue that same year announces that there were "more than 2,000 dancers at the Houston [Texas] Coliseum. The 171 spaces marked out for squares were all filled with overflow dancing off the floor at the first annual Houston Square Dance Festival. Bob Osgood, Al Brundage and Herb Greggerson were all present." The June issue that year mentioned the Third Annual Spring Roundup in Boise, Idaho and that the Square Dance

Association of Wisconsin issued its first State Association Handbook[4]. The Spokane Festival for teens drew more than twenty-five hundred teen dancers with "Red" Henderson, supervising.

## GROWTH IS RAPID - BUT HARD TO QUANTIFY

Few reliable indicators of growth are available but there are some firm numbers that give us an idea of the situation in the early years. One is the attendance figure for the National Square Dance Convention. This event has evolved to serve primarily modern, club dancers and was first held in Riverside, California in 1952. Attendance the first year was reported as roughly 6,000 over the three-day event. That probably means the actual count was about 3,000 since people were counted again each day they attended. The number of dancers at the National Convention grew more or less steadily to a peak in 1983 of 30,953 (if we drop out the highly unusual 39,796 that attended in 1976, the U.S. Bicentennial Year.) The growth pattern is not a straight line in part because the Convention moves each year to a different location. The actual number of people in attendance is not directly comparable, either, because the counting basis was not consistent. The density of the dancer population in the local area surrounding the National Convention location has a substantial impact on the actual attendance. The attendance figure does, however, give a clear indication that the popularity of the new form of square dancing was growing.

Another indicator that shows how rapidly this activity was expanding is the growth in the number of clubs and associations of clubs. The club form of organization was also a clear indicator of the distinction between the old and the new way of square dancing. While there were a few clubs providing the traditional style of square dancing in the late 1940's, there were none I can find that continued that program during the next decade. Traditional square dancing never disappeared but the rapid growth of the modern style overshadowed the remnants of it dramatically.

A selection of items from the 1953 issues of *Sets in Order* gives a sense of the broad expansion of clubs and festivals across the North American Continent during the early 1950's.

---

[4] The history of square dancing in Wisconsin has been traced in detail in an excellent book published in 1998. *Square Dancing in Wisconsin A Historical Anthology*, by Agnes Thurner is available from the author whose address is 1711 W. Fiesta Ln. Mequon, Wisconsin 53092

February 1953 - The Federation of Western SD Clubs of Detroit with 6 member clubs held a dance with live music.

February 1953 - The Kansas and the Indiana Square Dance Callers' Associations were formed.

March 1953 - The Fifth Annual Southern Arizona Square Dance Festival was held in January.

March 1953 - The First annual Western New York Square Dance Jamboree was held.

April 1953 - The second meeting of the Connecticut Square Dance Callers & Teachers Association is held. The 2nd annual meeting of the Greater Hartford [Connecticut] Square Dance Club was held in January.

April 1953 - The monthly Listing of square dance events shows three 1st annual events. These are in Tampa, Florida, Burbank California and Houston Texas. Three 2nd annual events are included in Provo Utah, Trinidad Colorado and Sheridan, Wyoming. A 3rd annual event is listed in Baldwin Kansas as is a 4th annual event in Butte, Montana. Two 5th annual events appear in St. Louis Missouri and Shreveport Louisana.

June 1953 - A full page listing Canadian square dance activities describes about a dozen clubs in Edmonton and surrounding areas. It also mentions that Earle Park of Yorkton, Saskatchewan calls for an adult and a teen club. The Folk Dance Federation in Winnipeg, Manitoba includes a modern club and a once-a-month "workshop." The final paragraph mentions that the British Columbia Callers' Association is sponsoring a series of four dances featuring callers from Seattle. Another article describes the 1st Jamboree in Cedar Rapids Iowa

July 1953 - The listing of events mentions the 3rd annual festival in Yuma, Arizonia, the 3rd annual Northwest District Festival in Enid Oklahoma and the 5th annual Festival in Omaha, Nebraska with 2400 dancing and 6200 watching. An article mentions that twenty-one members attended a callers' meeting in Shelley Idaho.

September 1953 - An article is included about square dancing in Okinawa with callers all in the U.S. military. It mentions formation of the club there in 1951.

The very complete history book, *Steps in Time*, published by the North Texas Square Dance Association (NORTEX) in 1985 shows the startup dates for most of the clubs in that area. In 1954 Dallas was host to the third National Square Dance Convention (NSDC) with an attendance of 5354. There were about ten clubs in the area at that time. By 1965 when the

NSDC was again held in Dallas the attendance was 13,196 and the number of clubs in the area was more than thirty. The NORTEX association was formed in mid-1961 with twenty-one member clubs. By the end of the first year nine more clubs had joined. Growth of the association was then steady with three or four clubs joining each year. The period of maximum growth in that area was the decade of the 1970's during which an average of five new clubs were formed each year. Membership in the association reached a peak of 163 clubs in 1981.

Another indicator of the rate of club formation is available from the pages of *The New England Caller* magazine. One of the principal reasons for starting this publication was to provide a listing of square dance events. Most of the clubs in the area where I was calling advertised their dances in the magazine each month. The magazine started in August 1951 with twenty pages that were 4-1/4-inches by 7-inches. By 1958, the January issue had thirty-four pages and in 1963 the page size had grown to 5-inches by 9-inches and there were 104 of them. When my first club, the Allemande 8's, was formed in Manchester, New Hampshire in 1956, there were only three other clubs in the North-of-Boston area. They were The Minutemen in Lexington, Massachusetts, the Trails End Reelers in Sanbornville, New Hampshire, and the Down East Western Square Dance Club in Kittery, Maine. In the January 1958 issue, there were ads for four dances in this area. The January 1963 issue listed ten dances in the same area and by January 1965, the number had grown to twenty-one.

In 1957 an association of square dance clubs called the Eastern District Square and Round Dance Association (EDSARDA) was formed in New England. They first published what was to become an annual Directory in January 1958. It listed forty-six clubs in Massachusetts. The 1967 edition listed seventy clubs in Massachusetts. In both Southern and Northern California there were similar associations that were formed in the early 1950's. It is virtually certain that the pattern in Southern California was the model for square dance growth in nearly all areas of the U.S. and Canada. The modern form had begun there and most of the rest of the areas followed that pattern a few years later.

While the club form of square dance organization and growth appears to have begun most vigorously in Southern California it was not copied exactly in other areas. Across the continent there were several ways of organizing square dance clubs' programs. In some areas a club usually danced once a week or twice a month to the same caller. He or she (although in the early days there were very few women) was the "club" caller and was the only

caller that most of the members ever danced to. Occasionally a club hired
one of the traveling callers to call a special dance and invited other clubs in
the area to join in supporting that dance. In some areas there were no "club"
callers and the club hired a different local caller for each dance. The
common format in New England became a weekly or biweekly club dance
on a weekday with the club caller. These clubs then also held a once-a-
month Saturday dance with a "guest" caller.

Important services provided by the clubs were recruiting new dancers and
sponsoring classes. Arrangements for these also differed from one area to
another. Some classes were sponsored by the club but run entirely by the
caller. In other areas the club caller was hired to teach a class that was
organized and supported by the club. Even in areas where different callers
were hired for each dance, clubs usually hired a single caller to teach the
class. Control over the class varied widely from one area to the next
although, within a region, the arrangements tended to be very similar.
Southern California clubs usually hired a different caller for each night.
Northern California clubs had a "club caller" who called their weekday
dances but for two or three "hoedowns" each year clubs hired traveling
callers from other areas. In many regions the allocation of Saturday nights
throughout the year among the various clubs for hoedowns became an
important function of the area association.

The club is the core of modern square dancing. In nearly every region clubs
were managed by an executive board of some sort. Even though many clubs
were formed by callers, it was usual for the management to be turned over to
a committee of dancers. Clubs were strong social units. Membership
involved participation that came in many forms. Almost as important as the
dancing in many groups was the refreshments that were served at the
dances. Every member was expected to contribute to the refreshment table.
The quality of the refreshments served at the club dance was a matter of
considerable pride.

Participation in the management of the club was both an important
responsibility and a social reward. Executive committees usually met once
a month and often included ten or twelve couples. In addition to the usual
officers there were chair couples for refreshments, recruiting, publicity,
programming parties, hiring guest callers, running the classes, welcoming
guests and a variety of other responsibilities. Executive committee meetings
were both a place to accomplish the business of the club and a social event.

Square dance clubs were unique social entities. There were (and still are) very few activities that involved couples participating together. Square dancing was a wonderful place for couples to meet other couples, to make friends that were "our friends" rather than "his friends" or "her friends." Complete strangers who met on the first night of square dance class have formed lifelong friendships.

The club's social impact extended well beyond the dance nights. One of the most striking illustrations of this effect is evident in the early days of the Friendly Mixers, a club in Rhode Island. Their caller, Lloyd Platt, worked four or five nights a week for that one club. He taught both a square dance class and a round dance class. (In the 1950's most round dance teaching was done by callers.) He also called a "workshop" once a month where club members learned new dance routines and calls, a twice-each-month round dance party and twice a month he called a Saturday night party dance with both squares and rounds. Members of the club shared their other interests, too, and formed a club bowling team, a card group and a sailing group. Lloyd and his wife, Marge, also ran a group for children sponsored by the Parent Teachers Organization in town to which many of the club members brought their children. In addition to being the dance leader for the group, the Platts were a focal point for the social activities of the group as were many club callers of that time.

A common practice with square dance groups was the after-party. When the hall and refreshments had been cleaned up, the party often moved to continue at someone's home. Hosting the after-party had a tendency to become a point of social competition and including the caller among those present escalated the prestige of the host couple. For the caller and partner, most of whom held full-time jobs in addition to their calling, the additional time commitments could become a problem. This was particularly true when the caller worked for more than one club. Fortunately, most of us were younger then and could tolerate the continuing late nights better than we might today.

## MORE CLUBS MEAN MORE CALLERS

The expanding number of clubs created a demand for more callers. An important element of every club program was the square dance class. In the 1950's a class that taught everything a new dancer needed to know could be completed in ten weeks or less. The first class that I taught was in 1955 as we formed the Allemande 8's in Manchester, New Hampshire. It was six weeks long and I spent the last night reviewing because I had taught all the calls then in regular use - a total of about twelve. I don't have the program for that first class but I do have the program for the class in the fall of 1956 which started on October 20. On the first night I taught: Dos a Dos, Swing, Allemande(s), Grand Right & Left, Ladies Chain, Right & Left Thru and Stars. The second night I taught All Around and See Saw, Dos Paso, Pass Thru, how to make lines, Split the Ring and Alamo Style Balance. The third night program worked the calls already taught in both goal post and route (facing line) arrangements and added Allemande Thar. That was effectively the end of the calls that were taught in class. These terms were then used in slightly different ways in the dance routines that I had memorized and I reviewed the entire routine for the dancers each time before I called it. We did add the standard breaks of the day, Allemande O, Triple Allemande, Red Hot and Daisy Chain but each was a combination of various hand turns and was called directionally each time.

It was usual for clubs to offer two classes each dance season. The season varied depending on location. In California, clubs danced every week all through the year. In New England, the club season matched the school year. Callers were kept busy a couple of nights a week. As new clubs were formed, the available callers found themselves busier than they wanted to be. Most were calling as an avocation or even, with less compensation, as a hobby. They had full-time jobs to keep.

The increase in the number of callers and the formation of caller organizations paralleled the increase in the number of clubs. Clearly the two growth patterns were related to each other. New callers were needed for the new clubs but it was also true that the expanding dancer population inevitably spawned a few folks who found calling appealing. New clubs were formed because dancers wanted a group closer to where they lived. Conversely, some groups were formed by new callers who wanted a group of their own. The North Texas Callers Association was formed in 1960, a year before the NORTEX dancers' association was formed. In New England, the Eastern District Square and Round Dance Association (EDSARDA) started in 1959 and it was with their encouragement that the New England Council of Callers Associations (NECCA) came into existence in 1962. As the name implies there were already local associations of callers throughout the area. NECCA was to be a representative body with delegates from each of the local associations.

My own local association, Tri-State Callers Association, was formed in 1960. It was the first of several caller organizations that I helped to get started. Three of us, Joe Casey, myself and Warren Popp, were the most active callers in the area that included parts of Massachusetts, New Hampshire and Maine. We could see a rapid influx of new callers and new clubs in the region and we were concerned that differences in teaching and in program would inhibit the interaction between dancers and clubs that we felt would be good for square dance growth. We got together one day at the kitchen table in Warren's house in Amesbury, Massachusetts, discussed these concerns and agreed to try to arrange a monthly meeting of the callers who were active in the area. The association was formed in 1960 with about twenty members.

It is as difficult to find firm numbers to accurately show the growth in the number of callers as it is to show the growth in numbers of dancers. NECCA first published a directory of callers in 1964. It listed 284 in the New England area. The second directory in 1966 listed 352. We know that in 1956 there were four callers doing the modern style of calling in that same North-of-Boston area where my first club was formed. There were another half dozen calling the traditional style but most of them were not members of the newly-forming caller associations and were not included in the directory. A check of the callers in that same area in the 1966 directory showed that the four had grown to fifty-nine.

Jon Jones, the first president of the North Texas Caller's Association, wrote a report of the history of that organization in 1995 from which we get an idea of the rate of increase in the caller population of that area. He notes that when he started dancing in the mid 1950's there were about twenty callers. Jon and C.O. Guest collaborated in forming the association in 1960. Within a couple of years, the membership had doubled and by the early 1970's it had more than doubled again to about 100 members.

With considerable help from Debbi Bliss, widow of caller Nate Bliss who was one of the early members, I have developed a reasonably complete history of the membership in the Northern California Callers Association. It started in 1949 with forty-eight members and grew rapidly to a peak of 368 in 1958. Since then a slow but steady decline reduced the membership to 175 in 1969, 148 in 1978 and less than 100 in 1989. Some of this decline may be traceable to the startup of the Santa Clara Valley and other Associations overlapping the area that was initially in the Northern California Association territory.

# CHAPTER 5 - CHOREOGRAPHY CHANGES

In 1959 I drove to Colorado to attend Ed Gilmore's school for callers. I had just started teaching dancers to call and I wanted to see how a caller school was run. Things were happening but, unfortunately, the curriculum at Ed's caller school didn't reflect the differences in dance styles around the country. Talking with the other students who came from a widespread area of the western U.S. did enlighten me considerably. The differences also showed up clearly in *Sets in Order*. The contrast between the modern and the traditional forms of square dancing was increasing rapidly. Most striking of the choreographic distinctions was the hand-turn action of the Allemande breaks. Creation of the call Dos Paso at the Shaw institute in 1949 and an increasing use of Star actions led to a type of choreography that was definitely not a part of traditional square dancing. Allemande Thar which had been invented before World War II as a demonstration figure was the first of the Allemande breaks. It started as a complete dance routine but callers soon learned to use just one part of the full routine and combine it with Dos Paso and other hand-turn actions into changing sequences. A full alphabet of "allemande breaks" was published in the June 1951 issue of *American Squares*. The list started with Allemande A which began "Allemande Left for an Allemande A, a right and a left for a Half Sashay and continuing to Allemande X which started "Allemande Left and Allemande X, It's a right and a Left and Swing the next." That last one was attributed to Jim York who was a prolific writer of choreography. The alphabet was completed with "Y" and "Z" which were poems that did not include directions for the dancers.

These circle actions were the first choreographic situations in which callers found they could change routines and still keep track of the dancers. As long as they didn't do a Two Ladies Chain, the order of the dancers - what we later came to call "sequence" - didn't change. A caller could move dancers clockwise or counterclockwise with respect to their partners and still get them back together easily. If any man got back to his partner, they were all matched. This was the beginning of "sight" calling.

Most callers, however, were not inclined to experiment. We were still learning sequences of calls that we found in print or heard other callers use. Variations came largely in the way we combined these learned routines. We used two different "figure" routines and three different "breaks" in a single tip. Figures were actions that had two "active" couples and two "inactive" couples although this was not really a true distinction. It served to distinguish between the figure and the break that was a circle type action with all the dancers doing all the parts of the routine the same way. Figures were still variations on the goal post and route patterns that we discussed in Chapter 3.

Another variety was being introduced in modern square dancing by the invention of new calls. One of the first that made a significant change in the choreography was the call Square Thru that appeared first in *Sets in Order* in 1956. I remember very clearly my first encounter with this call. It was in 1957 at a square dance weekend run by Al Brundage with Lee Helsel (from Sacramento, California) on the staff. Lee taught the call early in the weekend and it became a substantial part of the weekend choreography. I remember it being quite complicated and difficult to learn. I also know that I spent the next couple of years teaching it to dancers wherever I called. We did it in many different forms. Fractions were part of the first teach but the left handed and split variations were much more complicated. I used Square Thru and its variations as the basis for a full three-hour workshop session on several occasions during the late 1950's.

A call that had an impact nearly equal to that of Square Thru and was introduced at about the same time was Dixie Chain. That call didn't last into today's choreography although it was used during the late 1950's and into the 1960's almost as much as Square Thru. In 1968 when *Sets in Order* assembled a Gold Ribbon Committee to assess the most popular calls then in use it was included, but by 1976 when the CALLERLAB Mainstream Program was established, Dixie Chain was not included. The action of the call started like a Ladies Chain. The right hand person in two facing pairs took right hands and moved past each other to take left hand with the opposite left hand person. They then passed by and the original left hand persons took right hands and passed each other to end standing behind their original partner. A variation that stopped the action before the original left hand people passed each other and ended, instead, in an Ocean Wave has survived into today's choreography. It is Dixie Style to an Ocean Wave.

It is interesting to speculate on the reason that this very popular call didn't remain in regular use. One theory, suggested to me by Johnny Wedge, a caller from Massachusetts, is that the call was particularly useful in the goal post type of choreography. As we will show later in this chapter, that style of choreography also faded from popularity during the same time period. The box formation, Chicken Plucker type of choreography that replaced it was not well suited to the use of the Dixie Chain action.

Another new call that had a lasting impact was Wheel & Deal. It appeared in *Sets in Order* in 1960 as an example of an "experimental" call. The *5-Year Book* also included a definition of a "basic" which is instructive to note.

> A basic is a NECESSARY movement with a SHORT clear call that cannot otherwise be given "descriptively" in the time needed. The call should not be confused with the sound of other calls. The movement itself should not be one that could be called just as well with existing basics (calls.) The movement should be smooth flowing (not erratic or awkward) and should lend itself to rapid teaching. Last, to be considered a basic, a movement must prove its ability to withstand the test of time thru continued usage.

Wheel & Deal clearly met this test of time but many others that were created during this era failed. There was a series of calls created at about the same time that had names suggesting gambling. Shuffle the Deck was one, Acey Deucy was another, but the only one to withstand the test of time was Wheel & Deal. While Square Thru had taken several years to become accepted to the point that it was included in nearly every modern square dance program, Wheel & Deal accomplished this within no more than a year.

The Sets in Order *Year Book of Square and Round Dancing No. Two* published in 1958 and covering material from the 1957 issues of the magazine gives us a view of choreography as the growth of modern square dancing accelerated. It had changed in some very significant ways. The list of calls in common use when the magazine began publication in 1949 was quite short, somewhere around a dozen. *Year Book...No. Two* contains a glossary of terms. It is included, the editor's say, "because today's square dancers dance together more and more in each other's home areas." The list includes definitions for about 125 terms. About 100 are words that callers use to direct dancer actions and about twenty-five fit the definition of a basic given above. The rest are dancing routines that have been given names or are descriptions of regional differences in styles of dancing. The allemande breaks "A" and "O" and description of different ways of doing Do Sa Do or Docey Do are examples.

This comparison suggests that there had been a growth in the call vocabulary from somewhere around a dozen calls in 1950 to twice that number in 1957. It was still true that new calls were being introduced at a moderate pace. That, however, was about to change. Over the next decade the rate of new call introduction exploded right along with the increase in the dancer population. By 1960 we had added three calls that were accepted by square dancers nearly everywhere; Square Thru, Dixie Chain and Wheel and Deal. Other calls were proposed but they didn't receive the acceptance that these three achieved.

New calls would not only add to the vocabulary of square dancing; they also started to change the basic patterns of square dance action. In the early 1950's, choreography involved some variations on the visiting couple style of dances and a great deal of swinging. There was a very limited list of calls and the breaks were nearly all circle actions and Grand Right and Left. By the mid-1950s, the goal post pattern was common and variations on the facing line type of action known as the route were also regularly called. Introduction of Box the Gnat and later Square Thru led to a new choreographic pattern that would last to this day.

That new choreographic pattern appeared in 1957 in a dance with the name Chicken Plucker written by Bill Shymkus from Chicago. This dance was:

> First and third bow and swing, go up to the middle and back again.
> Forward again and pass thru, split the ring and around one.
> Into the middle, pass thru and circle four, half way around and dive thru
> Pass thru and right and left thru, turn your girl and you dive thru
> Pass thru and a right and left thru, and turn your girl like you always do
> Dive to the middle and a right and left thru
> Turn your pretty girl and you circle up four
> Half way around to the rhythm of the band,
> Pass Thru to a left allemande, left allemande, etc.

The goal post routine in this dance was in common use by then and is used to set up the Dive Thru, Pass Thru, Right and Left thru action across the set. Like the circle break action, this routine was easy for the caller to keep track of. As long as there were no Two Ladies Chain actions, the Dive Thru, Pass Thru, Right and Left Thru could be repeated indefinitely and the caller needed only to return the number one man to his home place to be sure the Allemande Left would be with the original corner for everyone.

Box the Gnat[5] provided another way to set up this basic pattern. First the caller used Box the Gnat, Face Partner and Pass Thru. The next step was Head Couples Half Sashay then Box the Gnat and Face the Sides and, finally, Square Thru left the active couples facing the outsides to start the Right and Left Thru, Dive Thru, Pass Thru action that is the essential part of this pattern. However it was set up, callers quickly learned that they could tease the dancers by repeating the action leading to the Allemande Left several times before they actually called the Allemande. The excitement and tension built by withholding the Allemande was tremendous and the dancer response when the Allemande was finally called seemed almost an explosion.

For the 2001 CALLERLAB Convention I put together a program called "Dancing in the 1960's." It was based on the core patterns that were the foundation of dancing in that period. The invitation that I wrote to the callers who presented that program described the choreographic situation in 1960 this way:

> The choreography of this period was built around a few very standard frameworks. Callers created variations - most of them written out and memorized in complete detail - based on these standard choreographic patterns. Many...who were calling during that period in square dance history will recognize the names of these patterns; names like Whirlwind, Chicken Plucker, Texas Star, Goal Post Choreography.

The handout given to those who came to that dance described one of the most exciting and challenging dance patterns of the day with these words:

---

5 The action of Box the Gnat has a man and woman change places by joining right hands with the woman turning under the man's arm.

## HAND TURN HASH

This was not a specific routine. It was the first type of choreography in which callers resolved the routine by watching the dancers. The action was forward and backward in the Grand Right & Left mixed in with fractional stars and Dos Paso. Since there were no changes of sequence, resolving the square required only that one man be returned to his original partner.

Another new call that made a fundamental change in the structure of modern square dancing was Swing Thru and it didn't arrive on the scene until 1962. Before Swing Thru we did make ocean waves with a Dos a Dos to a wave but it was very difficult to get the dancers out of those waves. We always did a Balance in the wave after the Dos a Dos but there were very few options after the Balance. One example from the 1961 Year Book (No. 6) illustrates this point. The caller directed the center dancers in the wave (the ladies) to make an arch and the ends to duck through that arch and U-turn back for a Right & Left Thru. We also called arm turns directionally saying "turn half by the right then half by the left" for the action of the Swing Thru call. There was, however, no easy action to call from a wave formation and thus the formation was little used. Swing Thru was also the first of what we can describe as compound calls. By this term I mean a call that combined two or more actions that had been called individually into a single action with a unique name. In the case of Swing Thru I remember Ed Gilmore assuring me that the term would never last because we could very well describe the action with directional calls and thus had no need for the term.

Ed was wrong. Swing Thru has become as much a core action in modern square dancing as Square Thru. Both calls led to fundamental changes in the pattern of dance action in modern square dancing. Modern callers can hardly imagine square dancing without both of these calls. It is interesting, however, to note how slowly Swing Thru was accepted into the common vocabulary. In the December 1968 issue of *Sets in Order* the Workshop section included seven pages of choreographic material from a half dozen callers. The call Swing Thru appeared only four times even though the Gold Ribbon Committee's list of Extended Basic calls published a month later did include Swing Thru. Also included on the Extended Basic list were two calls, Run and Trade, that were created within six months after Swing Thru to make it easier for callers to work with the ocean wave formation.

In the late 1960's, however, callers were not improvising choreography very much. The widespread use of any new call took time to develop. Until the choreographic creators had written and published routines using the new terms most callers were unable to add them to their programs. Square Thru was relatively easy to integrate into the goal post choreography that we were already using when it was added to the vocabulary. Swing Thru, on the other hand, required a much more substantial choreographic change. It was difficult to use without the complementary calls Run and Trade. Together they made a very different type of dance routine. One illustration of the extent of that change is the Two-Faced Line formation created by the combination Swing Thru and the Centers Run. That new formation brought about a change in the description of the Wheel and Deal so that it could be called from the new formation.

# CHAPTER 6 - NEW CALLS AND CHOREOGRAPHY MANAGEMENT

In the early 1960's, square dance choreography had started to change. The introduction of new calls was accelerating and would continue at a furious pace for the next twenty years. The standard formations were solidly in place and would remain the basis of modern square dancing for at least fifteen more years. During the 1960's, however, several callers began to write about methods of choreography management. These eventually produced a substantial change in the experience of square dancing for the crowds of new participants that were filling halls all over North America.

As the decade changed from the 1950's to the 1960's, square dances were usually complete dance routines that the callers had memorized and called without much variation. The circle type of break allowed callers to incorporate unpredictable routines and keep the dancers paying careful attention but the dance patterns themselves were repeated in much the same way each time they were called. The Chicken Plucker routine could be varied pretty easily without much risk of losing track of the dancers. The principal variation, however, was in how many times the active couples were moved across the square. A Two-Ladies-Chain type of action was avoided in all but completely memorized routines. The breaks between figures could be improvised, since there were no Ladies-Chain type of actions and no sequence-changing actions in the circular break patterns. A caller could return everyone to their partner in the correct order to promenade home just by getting one man back to his partner. In the figure between breaks, however, the pattern usually started with an action that changed at least the sequence of the men and the routine often included actions that exchanged ladies as well. The only variation possible with routines like these was to include more than one of them in a tip.

Starting with the publication of *The Keys To Calling Square Dances* by Bob Dawson and Don Bell in 1961, and *Instant Hash* by Rickey Holden and Lloyd Litman in 1962, there were several books written that began to explore the organization or structure of dance choreography. These also described methods that a caller could use to change a memorized routine or create an unplanned routine as they called without losing track of the dancers. A dance routine was only successful if, when it was completed, the dancers could execute the Allemande Left with their original corner so they could promenade home in the proper order (sequence). Three major and different methods of choreographic management were developed during the decade of the 1960's.

## MODULES

The most widely adopted of the methods used by callers to reduce their memorization workload was what has come to be known as the "module" system[6]. In *Instant Hash*, the authors discussed "analysis" of choreography and introduced the terms "zero" and "equivalent." They pointed out that any complete dance routine is also a "zero" which they define as a set of calls that return the dancers, after completion, to the same place they were when the routine began. In their earliest form, callers used complete routines as "zeros" when they started using more than a single memorized routine in a complete tip. The next step may have been the realization that in the goal-post routine the action in the middle after the active couples had done the Pass Thru, Around One to the middle could be changed each time the routine was called.

In *Instant Hash* Holden and Litman said "...*the basic principle of hash* is this: Take four beginnings or set-ups, four middle parts and four endings or ways to get out of formations and you may create sixty-four figures using only twelve parts." That summation of what was soon to be known as the

---

[6] The use of the word "module" did not begin until much later. I have not been able to find any reference before 1970 that used the word in the way we use it today to describe a set of calls that is less than a complete dance. Bill Peters used the term "Magic Module" in 1973 to identify a routine that he described in his *Choreo Breakdown* note service. That may have been the first use of the term as it is used today.

"zeros and equivalents" method of choreographic control is without question the beginning of today's "module" method.

I remember very clearly my first realization of a module that did more than return the dancers to the same place they had started. In the late 1950's, many singing call figures started with a series of Ladies Chain actions; things like "Head Ladies Chain Across and the Side Ladies Chain to the Right" or "Side Ladies Chain to the Right and the New Side Ladies Chain Across." In 1960 I went to Al Brundage's Funstitute Square Dance Vacation week at West Point in New York. Lee Helsel, from Sacramento, California was on the staff and I was discussing singing calls with him. During that conversation he pointed out to me that all that the Ladies Chain "setup" did was to give each man his corner or right hand lady for a partner. The singing call routine then returned the dancers to their partner and a corner or right hand lady progression had been accomplished. Today, as I write this, callers and dancers alike would probably regard this revelation as no big deal. For me at the time, with ten years of calling experience, it was an earthshaking discovery.

Throughout the early decades of modern square dancing, it was common practice for the caller to walk the dancers through a routine before it was called to be sure that everyone understood what was expected of them. To walk the dancers through a singing call routine most callers had been including the "set-up" action in the walk through. Recognition that the set-up was common to many routines and did not have to be included in the walk through was an important realization. From there it was a short jump to showing dancers only the part of the routine that was not familiar. That technique carried through the endless flood of new calls introduced during the twenty years after 1960. As mentioned earlier, it was a simple matter for the caller to create "zero" modules using the new calls and insert them into the Chicken Plucker routine or one of the other standard choreographic routines of the day. It was a small step from inserting zero modules to the recognition that a module could also be made to equal or take the place of another call or group of calls. In the Chicken Plucker routine, the Right & Left Thru could be replaced with a module that accomplished the same thing - an equivalent.

**SIGHT**

The first documentation of the Sight method of managing choreography was in one of the first books to recognize that it was possible to do something other than memorizing a complete routine. *The Keys To Calling Square*

*Dances* by Bob Dawson and Don Bell was published in 1961 and offered a detailed presentation of the important elements of the method. In a section headed "PRELIMINARY BASIC CONCEPTS" they set out a ground rule that prohibits "SPECIAL COMMANDS" which are listed as calls "addressed specifically to:

1. Any one person.
2. Any one couple.
3. One Side and one Head person.
4. One Side and one Head couple."

They go on to point out that such calls would be acceptable if they were "canceled out" by a later call in the same routine. The section goes further to make clear that the consequence of "Special Commands" is to violate the clockwise or counterclockwise order of men and/or women.

In the same section they make clear that when special commands are avoided the men must be either IN SEQUENCE or OUT of SEQUENCE. The section continues under the heading IT CAN'T BE ANY OTHER WAY! to say:

> No matter what movements are executed with the square, the position of the individuals in one set of adjoining couples (one Head and one Side couple) will ALWAYS exactly duplicate the position of the other individuals in the pair of adjoining couples (the other Head and Side couple.) One set of couples is a MIRROR IMAGE of the other and it can't be any other way!

This is an expression of the concept that would later be called Symmetry. It's interesting, as an aside, to note that this is probably the origin of the "Mirror Image" terminology that would, three decades later, become a matter of lengthy discussion within the CALLERLAB Caller Training Committee. You see, in fact, the two couples are NOT a mirror image of each other for the same reason that, for a man looking in the mirror, the part in his hair moves from the left side of his head to the right (or vice versa) and a left hand, viewed in a mirror, appears to be a right hand. Nevertheless, Dawson and Bell correctly observe that this balance between the two halves of the square "means that a caller can completely ignore one half of the square and concentrate attention on only four dancers."

Starting with the description of these concepts, the authors continue to discuss the importance of "position" which they identify as the relative arrangement of the men and the women in a formation. The current official

CALLERLAB term for this "position" is Arrangement. Thus, in the Preliminary Basic Concepts section of this book Dawson and Bell have identified three of the four choreography conditions that are recognized today. They are Formation, Arrangement and Sequence. They have also established the concept of Symmetry. With these concepts established, they go on to present a set of methods for "RESOLVING THE SQUARE." Clearly, this book is the first complete documentation of the Sight method of choreography management.

Many people, including Les himself, have identified Les Gotcher as the originator of "Sight" calling. His book Les Gotcher's *Textbook of American Square Dancing*, which was also published in 1961, includes a section with the title "'Science of Sight' Teaching and Calling Methods." By today's understanding, the methods described in that section are not what we now refer to as "Sight" calling. He notes that there are "only three or four things about which we must acquire a thorough knowledge." He did identify the importance of symmetry and then he goes on to say "First, we must know at any given time just who is dancing with whom." Secondly, he says, "we must know whether or not the men are in sequence." The third thing Les says that we must keep in mind is the shape of the square and the placement of women with respect to men. These are all-important parts of choreographic management but do not comprise a method for control of these elements. While it was not a documentation of sight calling, Les Gotcher's book was one of the first places where the components of choreography were separated one from the other. Rickey Holden and Lloyd Litman produced the definitive work on that subject a year later in their book *Instant Hash* but Les' book did identify the components.

At an Al Brundage Funstitute at West Point in 1961 with Gotcher on the staff I had the opportunity to hear directly from Les how I could put his ideas to practical use. In writing the book he had the help of a daughter as consulting editor. Without her he was not as skilled in explanations. Although his attempt to describe a "system" of choreographic management was not easy to grasp, he helped me to think about a combination of calls - a module - in terms of what it did to the sequence of the men and the partner relationships in the square. For the first time I understood that, from facing lines of couples, the calls Half Square Thru, Trade By would change the sequence of the men and leave each man facing the opposite lady from the one he had as a partner in the line. (Note, also, that Trade By did not then exist as a call. The combination of the two actions was known by the name Barge Thru.) For me this was a dramatic change in the way I thought about dance routines.

## MENTAL IMAGE

Another of the choreographic control methods was eventually known as the Mental Image system. Its first complete description in print was by Jay King in his book *The Fundamentals of Calling,* published in 1968. The method was in use several years before the book was published, but I have not been able to establish beyond any question who invented it. Jay attended the caller school that I was teaching in New Hampshire in the early 1960's. I had not, at that time, heard anything about this method of choreographic control. I now know that callers in the south-of-Boston area were teaching and using what they called the "slot system" during the early 1960's. This was clearly the starting point for Jay's book. The trail leads back strongly to Dick Tilley from Holbrook, Massachusetts who taught many callers and was probably the one who introduced Jay King to this method of keeping track of the action in a square. I have also been told by Gloria Roth that her husband, Johnny, had invented the system "on the hood of a car" with a caller in southeastern Massachusetts whose name she thought was Tilley. I am comfortable in the understanding that Dick and Johnny shared the development of the early concepts of this method. They may have been extending a concept that was published in 1963 in the book *Build Your Hash* by Ed Michl. Ed, who lived in Ohio, described a process of moving the corner lady to different "spots" in the square as a preliminary to resolving to a Left Allemande. His system does not deal with change of sequence for either men or women and thus cannot be accepted as a true resolution method.

Wherever the system was invented, there is no question about the first documentation of the details of the system. In the introduction to his book, Jay lays out four rules. The third of these says "Call only those things that you can mentally dance as though you were the #1 man in an imaginary square..." It is probably from that rule that Jay derived the name Mental Image which he used as the name for the system in the 1972 edition of the book. The essential control element of the system is to move the location in the square of an "Allemande Position" by managing the use of partner-changing actions. Jay King, who had put himself through college writing children's books, was able to describe a learning process that beginning callers could understand and master. Although it depended heavily on the caller being able to visualize the movement of one man in the square through the pattern as it was called, the system also required a great deal of practice. Jay's book took a new caller through the vocabulary of calls one at a time, urging them to understand the effect of each call on the position of the key man in the square. We have since learned that this disciplined approach to understanding the action of each call is an essential part of learning to call well, regardless of the method of choreographic management being used.

Jay died in 1976. Gene Trimmer acquired the rights to his publications and continued to make them available for many years. I was asked to present (posthumously) the CALLERLAB Award of Excellence to Jay King in 1988. During my presentation speech, I asked all the callers there who had been influenced by Jay King as they learned to call to please stand. More than half of the nearly 500 callers present stood. The utility of the Mental Image system of choreographic management was diminished by the introduction of more complex calls. Several of these included a partner change in the action of the call and some also changed sequence of the men. Nevertheless, it is difficult to overstate the importance of both the method and the writings of Jay King on the development of modern square dancing.

One of the precursors of this method was a system invented, or at least documented, by Stan Burdick who became the owner/editor of *American SquareDance* magazine in 1968. His first publication of *The Windmill System of Hash Calling,* was in 1965. The Windmill system does contain some elements of today's Mental Image method as described in the CALLERLAB *Curriculum Guidelines for Caller Training Technical Supplement.* In particular, it is based on moving a key man to a particular position in the square to allow an Allemande with the correct corner in the proper sequence. It does not, however, take the next step of using the Ladies Chain and equivalents to change the location of that position. Another way of viewing this (Windmill) system is to recognize that it provides a dance pattern or framework into which a variety of modules (or sighted subroutines) may be inserted while allowing the caller to keep track of the movement of the dancers through the framework. That framework can be thought of and used in the same way that the Chicken Plucker routine is commonly used by a caller using the modular system.

Some use of modules caught on fairly quickly. Callers were accustomed to memorizing and the ability to interchange and combine memorized choreographic bits was a natural extension of that skill. The sight and mental image techniques were significant departures from what callers had been doing and they caught on much more slowly. In fact it would be another twenty years before a preponderance of the most successful callers was comfortable with sight calling. The mental image method had a wide but fairly short popularity. The learning system that Jay King advocated in his books gave callers a fundamental understanding of the choreographic consequences of each of the calls they were using. The extension of this understanding into a flexible choreographic control system required substantial additional study and practice. At the same time, the new call explosion introduced some that did not fit easily into the mental image system. Many callers used the Jay King learning system but, when they had built an understanding of the calls, found that the sight method offered an easier and more flexible control. Those callers who have mastered the mental image system find it immensely useful, particularly in singing calls. The principles of the mental image method of choreography management were explored more recently in the book *Out of Sight* published in 1983 by Don Beck. Don extended the concepts and methods of the system to show how to apply them with the newer, more complicated styles of choreography that had been developed since Jay's last rewrite. Don also explored the conceptual basis of the mental image method more completely than did Jay's books which were intended exclusively as "how to" manuals. This book has preserved the mental image system as a useful tool for callers even though few caller schools give the system more than a passing mention.

The idea that choreography should change and that dancers would enjoy the uncertainty of improvised dance patterns was introduced into the square dance activity during the 1960's. The idea was adopted and accepted slowly. Choreography that is created as it is called is the most important distinction between traditional and modern square dancing. While many have traced the origins of modern western square dancing back to the 1940's, the ability to change the pattern as the dancers executed it was not available before 1960 except for the hand-turn action in the breaks between figures. True flexibility and skill with this use of choreographic change were slow to become established. The real impact of it on the dancers was not to be felt until the late 1970's after CALLERLAB had standardized and won acceptance of the Mainstream list of calls.

# CHAPTER 7 - THE NEW CALL FLOOD

The rate of new call creation accelerated rapidly during the 1960's. In the December 1968 issue of *Sets in Order* the work of a "Gold Ribbon Committee" was first published. This was a committee of prominent callers that Bob Osgood established to try to bring some order to the exploding vocabulary of calls. In his editorial in that issue he said, "We checked another list of terms the other day that included virtually every 'Experimental Movement' introduced during the past dozen years or more, and were astounded by the total of more than 800." In 1970, Bill Burleson published the first edition of his Encyclopedia with 1679 calls listed. Seven years later the contents of this encyclopedia had grown to 2542 calls and by 1982 the number had grown to 4368. Although no caller used all of these calls, it was clear that callers would have to find a way to incorporate new material into their programs without having to memorize complete new routines for each one.

The most popular way of dealing with this problem was the module method. A new call could be combined with standard calls to create a "zero" module that left the dancers, after completion of the module, exactly where they had started. This module could then be inserted into any of the routines that a caller had memorized. The learning curve for callers was quite steep. They could create zero modules fairly easily and the need to memorize new routines began to diminish. With new calls available at rates approaching twenty to thirty every month, even the experienced dancers could be kept interested learning new calls while the need to provide new and interesting dance routines began to shrink in importance. The other choreography management techniques, mental image and sight, also allowed callers to insert new calls into their programs without having to memorize new dance routines. This new flexibility for callers had a major effect on the dancing experience for the dancers.

Nearly everyone agreed that variety and changing choreography were important. In the Introduction to *The Fundamentals of Calling*, Jay King wrote in 1968:

> When Herb Greggerson, along about 1948, started calling 'Pass Thru, split that ring and around just one,' the kind of square dance choreography we think of as 'modern' was born. In this kind of choreography, dancers learn only a number of 'basic' movements (instead of learning entire dance patterns as they once did) and the caller, by use of these basics, moves the dancers through a series of 'grid,' line and column patterns <u>toward an ending known only to himself</u>. While dancers have stopped memorizing dance patterns, however, callers still use large numbers of memorized routines which today's dancers can often figure out after one time through and can anticipate the movements if the routine is called a second time.

Jay's source for this observation was almost surely the Holden/Litman book *Instant Hash*. His analysis of the distinction between the modern and traditional styles of square dancing makes clear the state of mind of the modern callers. They were searching wherever they could to provide more variety for the dancers. It is certainly true that his description of the essence of modern square dance choreography is widely accepted. It is also true that an important component of this type of dancing was the variety that "unmemorized" choreography provided. Jay, however, was well ahead of his time. The ability to change choreography as it was called was not to become widespread for at least another decade. In the meantime, most callers were providing variety with memorized modules. The sequence of these modules within a tip was changed but the dancers had encountered most of the material before. The walk-thru was still common throughout the 1960's, 1970's and the early 1980's and the frequent use of newly created calls that had to be taught before they could be used also reduced the level of dancer uncertainty.

During the 1960's, these new calls were coming with increasing frequency. They seemed to provide dancers with a substantial share of the variety they appeared to want. Dancers didn't notice that the new calls were being used in the same routines. They were too busy trying to keep up with the new vocabulary. Callers learned, also, that teaching a new call had a tendency to equalize the dancing skills of newer dancers and those who had been dancing for several years. For callers one of the easiest routines to use with new calls was the Chicken Plucker pattern. After the Square Thru that set up the box formation, that routine allowed a new call zero module to be inserted returning the dancers to the same place. The Chicken Plucker routine was then resumed to move the active couple to the other side of the square where the module was repeated. The routine was then completed back to the Left Allemande. Dancers had variety with the new call and callers had only to remember one or two modules for each call to provide all the variety most of the customers could handle. This also made it possible for dancers to dance with a minimum of difficulty even when several new calls were introduced in a single evening.

Les Gotcher was, perhaps, the most widely-traveled caller of that period. He also made extensive use of the floor-equalizing value of the new calls. His dance program incorporated several new-call tips each evening. He would sometimes open an envelope he claimed to have just received with a new call description from someone. He then taught the call to the floor and used it for that tip. The success of that programming technique in maintaining the interest of experienced dancers while allowing newer dancers to keep up spread rapidly. It soon became the standard way of programming for traveling callers. It also meant that local callers had to (because they were urged by the dancers) re-teach in their clubs the calls that dancers had encountered at the weekend traveling caller dances. It took a long time before dancers started to understand that new calls came and went. In the beginning dancers thought they had to know each of the calls that traveling callers were using. By the 1970's experienced dancers began to realize that many calls they were taught never appeared again. But in the 1960's there was great pressure on club callers to keep dancers aware of the new vocabulary.

## NEW CALLS AND NOTE SERVICES

The volume of new calls soon presented new problems for callers. Keeping up with them was a challenge. The established magazines did what they could but the number of calls quickly overwhelmed them. Dancers would come back to the club after dancing to a traveling caller and try to explain the new calls they had been taught. This process resulted in many variations for each call. Callers needed a way to know in detail how other callers were teaching the calls. A new form of publication came into existence to meet this need the caller note service. One of the most enthusiastic users of the new-call technique for programming was Les Gotcher. He also realized that callers would need to know about the new calls and he began to publish a monthly newsletter in 1959. The Southern California Callers Association also made their *Workshop Notes* available to subscriber members from all over the country. These were the first steps along a path that was to become very well traveled over the next two decades.

Even before these publications started, the earliest traveling callers had set up a newsletter of their own. It was a very early forerunner of the caller note services but was very private and exclusive. Al Brundage made reference to it in his presentation of the CALLERLAB Milestone Award to Dr. Ralph Piper in March of 1997. He said:

> When the square dance activity was an infant, there were no magazines, note services, recordings or other methods of gathering information on square or round dancing. Pappy Shaw dreamed up the idea that if the activity was to survive, we needed a method of communication so that ideas and dance material could be shared by the leaders around the country. I was privileged to be one of the twelve leaders to be included in the 'Round Robin.' This consisted of one or two pages of ideas, gimmicks, new material, or just chit-chat about what was happening locally from each caller on the list. Pappy started it off, sent it to Ed Gilmore, and the idea was that the packet went around the complete loop about twice a year. When you received it, you had two weeks to digest it, make notes from it, add your contribution, and then mail it to the next person on the list. I received my packet from Bascom Lamar Lunceford who represented the Appalachian area and was full of ideas and material on our Southern Mountain Dancing. After adding my contribution, representing the New England area, I would send the 'Round Robin' along to Floyd Woodhull in Elmira, New York (his Blackberry Quadrille on RCA Victor was one of the best and earliest instrumental pieces of the day - and I'm sure there are some old timers here that still carry it in their record case.)

> Floyd would send it along to Ralph Piper and I recall with much humbleness and respect the orderly and highly informational contributions of the person you are about to meet.
> (Ralph Piper died in January of 2001)

Since the first visits to Pappy Shaw's by Brundage and Gilmore occurred in the late 1940's, the Round Robin that Al describes probably began soon after that. The only other early communication aimed specifically at callers was the *Sets in Order* Workshop section. The magazine had initiated the Workshop insert section for callers in 1952. Initially it presented complete dance routines but these, inevitably, began to include new call words that were being introduced by traveling callers. In addition to the Workshop section, *Sets in Order* introduced a feature called Experimental Lab during 1960. In these features, call definitions, and sometimes conflicting definitions for the same terms, were presented in detail usually including "in-action" picture sequences.

In the January 1969 issue, *Sets in Order* listed some of the best known of the caller note services with contact information for each. The listing included those published by both the Southern and Northern California Callers Associations, Les Gotcher's *Tips to Callers* which began in 1959, the *National Callers' Report* started by Willard Orlich in 1960. The *National Callers' Report* was distinguished by an "invitation only" subscriber list limited to 100. Willard Orlich also offered, on a less restrictive basis, the *National Associations Report* and the *Akron (Ohio) Area Association Notes*. *Hashing It Over*, started by Jay King in 1967, was also mentioned but Jack Lasry's *Notes for Callers* was very new having begun in 1968 and was not included in the list. A principal function for each of these publications was to keep their subscribers aware of new calls as they were introduced.

The note service business boomed during the 1970's. Sometimes these began as publications of callers associations on the model of the Northern and Southern California Association notes. The Santa Clara Valley Callers Association Notes published by Bill Davis is an example of this approach. The other model was a private publication like *Choreo Breakdown* put out by Bill Peters without an association sponsor. Whatever the model, there were a couple of dozen services. Their popularity was assured by the local callers' need to know about new calls before their customers heard them from traveling callers. Most of these services also included caller training material aimed at improving the skill level of the local caller.

# CHAPTER 8 - CALLER TRAINING

Caller training in the early 1950's was primarily a local process. A caller who had run out of available nights would help an interested dancer to learn to call. New clubs were often formed by dancers who were traveling further to get to their weekly or bimonthly club meetings. They recruited friends and finally built a big enough group to start a new club in their town. Sometimes it was a group that wanted to dance on a different night. Whatever the incentive, the new group needed a caller. Folks who wanted to try calling were not hard to find among the eager group of new dancers. The experienced callers were willing to help when they had filled all of their available time, and learning to call wasn't very complicated. In the December 1954 issue of *American Squares* magazine, the roving editor, Rickey Holden, wrote an article titled "The Technical Aspects of Square Dance Calling." He listed the responsibilities of the Caller in four categories: Technical, Professional, Moral and Social or Recreation. The first section reads, in its entirety:

> 1. Technical: These are pretty much black and white. You are either in rhythm or you are not; either you can be understood or you can not be. Either you know what is an allemande left or you don't.

Caller training focused on the leadership skills in the other three areas of responsibility (Professional, Moral and Social or Recreation.)

Learning to call wasn't really a big deal. As we can see from the notes for the 1949 Gilmore school in Chapter 3, learning to call was largely a process of memorizing enough dance routines to fill an evening. Dances were learned in their entirety and called without change exactly as they were learned. There was little in the way of technical skill to be taught. Enunciation and loudness were mentioned and teaching skills were also discussed. There was considerable emphasis on making the delivery of the memorized words fit the rhythm and phrase of the music. But technical subjects like choreographic management, smoothness and flow and timing that are included in today's caller training curriculum were mostly unknown and unmentioned.

## THE TRAVELING TEACHERS

The institutes run by Lloyd Shaw and Herb Greggerson were usually attended by callers with experience. The new local callers were often trained as apprentices by the most experienced callers in the area. California led the way in making caller training a more formal process. As noted in Chapter 3, Ed Gilmore taught a school for callers in 1949 offered by the recreation department in Redlands California. At that time he had been calling himself only two years. He was, however, doing a lot of traveling. He was regularly hired by groups of callers to teach. Rickey Holden traveled widely during the early 1950's and took part in caller training programs in many locations. His affiliation with *American Squares* magazine and his experience gave him credibility in that field. Herb Greggerson also traveled widely before he built his hall in Riudoso, New Mexico. Herb conducted a weekend clinic in Massachusetts in 1950 that was a major step toward the introduction of the western style of dancing into New England. Several of the most active callers of that time attended the clinic and went home with new ideas.

## REGIONAL CALLER SCHOOLS

Al Brundage was a leader in developing caller training programs. He was consciously and actively promoting the "new" style of square dancing in New England. He ran a dancer workshop once a month on Sunday afternoon and in the morning before these he offered a training program for callers. Both new callers and those traditional callers who wanted to learn the "western" style took part. In 1952 he taught a school in Vermont with Ed Durlacher who was solidly rooted in the traditional style of dancing. He also worked a school in Wisconsin with Ed Gilmore in 1953. At Al's Country Barn in Stepney, Connecticut, Frank Kaltman, who owned the Folkcraft Record Co., organized a school in the early 1950's that was accredited by the New York school system. The staff included Al and Rickey Holden and a primary purpose was to teach physical education teachers from the New York City school system who were being pressured to include square dancing in their classes.

Al Brundage and Earl Johnston started one of the first, and certainly the most successful callers school in Pittsfield, Massachusetts in 1961. It soon moved to the East Hill Farm resort in Troy, New Hampshire where it grew to offer two week-long courses each summer, one for experienced callers and the other for newer callers. That school continued in operation until the retirement of both Al and Earl. It was taken over in 1993 by Ken Ritucci and Randy Page, two callers who had started their careers as teenage students at the Brundage/Johnston school. The Troy, New Hampshire school became so popular that Al and Earl started another in Harrisonburg, Virginia to accommodate the growing number of students who were traveling to New Hampshire from the south and west.

A long running and successful school was started by Frank Lane and Earl Johnston in 1971 at a hall in Estes Park, Colorado where Frank called regularly each summer. Another was started by Johnny Davis and Dick Jones at Promenade Hall, a square dance center built by Rich & Marva Shaver in Merriville, Indiana. These three were among the earliest week-long, live-in schools following on the model established by Ed Gilmore in Glenwood Springs, Colorado. By the late 1960's Gilmore was also running schools in Ohio and Michigan. In addition to these dedicated schools, some training was available for callers at the dancer vacation institutes. Many of these included sessions for callers along with the dance program for the dancers. It is interesting to note, however that for most of the decade of the 1960's the only advertising for caller training schools in *Sets in Order* was for the Ed Gilmore schools.

Many caller training programs were run on a small scale by local callers. My own was such a program. I began by offering to teach callers in the evening after a once-a-month Sunday afternoon dance workshop that I ran at the Hayloft Barn in Chester, New Hampshire. Each month I would discuss one of the topics that I identified as most important and then let the students practice calling for each other while I offered critiques and suggestions for improvement. I still feel it was an especially satisfactory way to run a school. It never started and never ended. Many callers went through the whole series of discussions a couple of times and then often came back a couple of times each year after that for a refresher. Another fairly-local training program for callers was established as soon as Howard Hogue started his Square Acres hall in East Bridgewater, Massachusetts in 1953. Edith Murphy who was wheelchair bound was a very knowledgeable voice coach and helped many of the callers in the south-of-Boston area who got their start in calling at Square Acres. Earl Johnston taught a week-long school there with Edith and Jack Livingston during the mid-1950's. Dick Jones was one of the students in that school.

A long-running regional caller training program began in 1966 with a weekend institute in Nebraska taught by Harold Bausch. Jerry Junck attended that first institute and reports that there were about a dozen caller hopefuls in attendance. The program started Friday evening with a dance called by the students who were critiqued by Harold. Saturdays were devoted to instruction on the important calling skills, including a considerable emphasis on a sight calling line resolution technique known as the "friends and enemies" method. This would have been one of the very earliest training programs to offer any square resolving method. Most callers at that time were still using modules as their only method for choreographic improvisation.

In addition to the five day schools there were caller association training programs. In California both the Northern and the Southern California associations were formed in the 1950's with the training of new callers as an important purpose. In New England the Old Colony Callers Association was started in 1950. It is probable that one of its first acts was to sponsor the Herb Greggerson visit that we mentioned earlier. During the 1960's caller associations were formed throughout the United States and Canada. A primary motivation for the creation of most of these associations was to provide training for new callers. The exploding dancer population was creating a strong demand for callers and many interested dancers were curious about life behind the microphone. Clubs ran amateur caller nights where interested dancers could try their hand at calling. Some of the experienced callers were concerned about training their own competition. But most realized that everyone would benefit if the new callers did a good job of teaching new dancers. Some of the local associations brought in traveling callers to do afternoon, full day or even full weekend caller training sessions. Ed Gilmore was often hired by the callers association to do a clinic for callers on the Sunday following a Saturday night dance he called in the area. However, with all of these training options available it was still true, as Bob Osgood noted in a 1974 article that "The greatest number of callers in the activity today, after having made the decision to take up calling, have simply taught themselves. For many, square dance caller schools were not available and the most likely method of learning how was to simply listen to callers, in person, on record and on tape."

When I went to Ed Gilmore's school in 1959, I was also starting to teach some callers and in addition to learning more about calling, I wanted to see what he included in a week-long school. Gilmore was certainly the most active and recognized teacher of callers at that time and this was the only place where he taught a full-week school. He was also one of the most active of the traveling callers. It is interesting to note that this school, like the 1949 school for which we have the notes, focused heavily on delivery style and leadership along with pages of dance routines written out in full detail with every word of patter as well as the calls. It's also interesting to observe that the notes in 1959 were less than 1/3 of the length of those for his 1949 school. This probably reflects the easy availability of published dance routines in *Sets in Order* and other publications. The technical concepts of choreographic management were yet to be discovered. Square dancing was still based on a collection of learned routines that were danced in a very similar way each time they were called. In his instruction Ed Gilmore strongly emphasized that the organization of a patter call should be very similar to that of the singing calls. He was also beginning to become acutely aware of timing.

## THE CURRICULUM EXPANDS

By the late 1950's, I had run out of free nights. I was calling and teaching classes every week for three clubs. If square dancing was to grow in my area, it was clear that we would need more callers. I started teaching them. I had been calling for a decade and had some coaching from Ralph Page and Al Brundage. When I started teaching, I felt there wasn't much to be taught beyond where to find dance routines, how to memorize them and how to start a square dance club. My trip to Gilmore's school made me aware that there was more to it than that. Even his school couldn't anticipate the changes that would take place in the next decade. Both the flood of new calls and the growing interest in choreographic variety with the development of methods for improvising dance routines contributed to a revolution in caller education. As mentioned in Chapter 6, three books for callers were published at the start of the 1960's. Les Gotcher's *Textbook of American Square Dancing*, covered the non-choreographic aspects of calling in seven of his 140 pages. *Instant Hash* made no pretense of covering more than choreographic technology. Only *Keys to Calling Square Dances* made significant mention of subjects other than dance routines: personal attributes, voice usage, timing, programming, use of sound equipment and teaching.

I felt the need of a real textbook that dealt with all the subjects in more detail than the available books. In 1966 I published privately a 150-page mimeographed textbook for use in my caller training program. In the introduction I wrote:

> When I first began to teach people to call about seven years ago, I repeated the search I had made when I learned calling myself. I discovered that there was no book available from which to learn the fundamental elements of calling. So far as I can tell this is still true. There are books that go into choreography extensively and much has been written about music and tradition. You can read about the more advanced aspects of calling in many places but little has been written about the mechanical aspects of calling modern square dancing in terms that have meaning for the beginning caller.

The chapter headings were The Music and the Call, Choreography, Timing, Programming, Teaching, Equipment and Square Dance Club Administration. Twenty years later the CALLERLAB Caller Training Committee agreed on a curriculum for caller training. Ten subjects were established as essential. To those identified by me and by *Keys to Calling,* they added smooth dancing and body flow, ethics and leadership.

The schools and clinics that did exist began to present information about more than what dance routines to call. As the magazines incorporated more dance routines in their publications, there was no need for the schools to offer this kind of material. At the same time there was a growing realization that there was more to calling than memorizing a few routines and delivering them in a musical chant or melodic singing style. A series of articles by Ed Gilmore in the March, April and May 1970 issues of *Sets in Order* discussed the "Science of Calling." He started with the sound of the call and how to make the words fit the musical beat and phrase. He then went on to explain that timing matched the delivery of the call to the action of the dancers. He addressed the action of the dance explaining that callers must understand the dance formation consequences of the calls they delivered. The final scientific component mentioned in the articles was the "natural sequence of movements." This was limited to a discussion of the importance of hand availability sequencing.

In 1969 a very complete textbook for square dance callers was published by Bill Peters in San Jose, California. Bill had been teaching callers for several years and his "other" job was preparing resumes. His book *The Other Side of The Mike* was the first widely available textbook to offer full coverage of the modern square dance callers' craft. In the introduction Bill recognized the absence of a suitable text with these words "…there is as yet no one book that provides an…all-encompassing view of a modern square dance caller's <u>total</u> function." The book was a whopping 346 pages long and included chapters on Timing, Presentation, Showmanship, Teaching, Programming, Sound, Leadership and Singing Call Techniques.

The articles by Gilmore were the first steps toward a project that was near to Bob Osgood's heart. He was well aware of the scarcity of complete textbooks for caller training but, since he was not active in caller training, nor even in calling for modern square dances himself, he needed others to do the writing. He solicited articles from most of the active teachers of callers and published them regularly in the pages of *Sets in Order*. He recruited John Kaltenthaler and Bill Peters to help him identify both the subjects and the authors of these articles. He stated at the outset that he was preparing a complete textbook for caller training but he never would have guessed in 1970 that the book wouldn't be published until 1985. The full title was *The Caller Text -The Art and Science of Calling Square Dances.* Awareness of the technology of calling square dances and, indeed, the technology itself was developing slowly. Bob had a difficult time finding callers who had both the knowledge he wanted to include in his book and the ability to write it down so that others could understand it. Many of the best callers had learned their skills over time and by experience. They had no idea how to pass on that experience. Bob rewrote many of the articles that he received so that the rest of us could benefit from the knowledge of these performance masters.

## LEADERSHIP TRAINING

Bob Osgood recognized that caller interaction and leadership would be of crucial importance as the modern square dance activity developed. Whatever information was available was published promptly in his magazine but he knew that it reached a very small segment of the exploding dancer and caller population. He had brought together several of the most active and respected callers of the day who served both as friends and leaders. One or more of them appeared on the staff of most of the festivals, conventions and dancer institutes throughout the country. Between them they had contacts with a large share of the active callers of the day. With this advisory group, which included Ed Gilmore, Lee Helsel, Bruce Johnson, Arnie Kronenberger, Bob Page and Bob Ruff, a Leadership Conference for callers was held at the University of California at Los

Angeles (UCLA) in July 1964 just before the National Square Dance Convention, held that year in Long Beach, California. About fifty of us gathered there for a two-day discussion about square dancing and our responsibilities to it.

This leadership conference was not and did not pretend to be a school for callers. It did, however, include a significant share of the callers who were actively teaching others to call. It helped raise our awareness about how widespread the activity had become and the extent to which we could all benefit from increased cooperation and coordination. Most of those present at that meeting would also be present at the first CALLERLAB Convention a decade later. A repeat of that meeting was held the next year but, because the National Convention had moved to another location it did not have the broad representation from outside the area that was present at the first conference.

I returned home from that meeting with an increased awareness of the importance of leadership. I was married at that time to Clara, a professor of psychology at Boston University. She encouraged me to organize a meeting of the leading callers in New England. She believed that a meeting of these leaders could, with the guidance of group dynamics professionals, help us to work together more effectively. Charlie Baldwin, editor of *The New England Caller* magazine, helped us organize a two-day meeting that was held at East Hill Farm in Troy, New Hampshire at the end of January 1966. Twenty of the most active callers in New England at the time were there. The meeting was much more intense and interactive than the Los Angeles conference. It set in motion a spirit of respect and cooperation among the callers of New England and brought about a recognition of the importance of leadership that lasted for at least a couple of decades. Among those in attendance were the most respected of our leaders, Al Brundage, Charlie Baldwin and Earl Johnston. The most respected of other active callers were represented by Red Bates, Ted Perkins, Jay King and Joe Casey who were among the most experienced of the modern callers in New England at the time. The rest of the group was drawn from newer callers who were active and popular in the region.

# CHAPTER 9 - CLUB LIFE IS RICH

The number of square dance clubs grew rapidly throughout the 1960's. At first there was only one club in town - in any town. The fastest growth was in smaller towns and cities. In some metropolitan areas there were several clubs but the more common pattern was one club in each town. As they grew, clubs divided and spread out. Sometimes the division was based on location. People who were traveling from the east side of town to the west side wanted their own club so they didn't have to travel so far. Sometimes clubs divided because one member became a caller and lured some of the group off to start a new club. For any number of reasons, clubs multiplied.

Square dance clubs were social organisms. Founding members recruited their friends for the first class. Everyone recruited folks like themselves and most groups had a significant homogeneity, at least at first. Friendships grew strong. Square dancing was an absorbing activity. Class met every week for most of a school year. People who had not been accustomed to touching any other person for more than a handshake found themselves swinging someone else's wife and putting an arm around people of the same sex. Even hugging other people was encouraged. Various areas had different names for the action but the call to Yellow Rock your corner was widely accepted to direct a hug with the corner and it was used frequently. I was never comfortable using the term unless I had arranged the dancers so their original partner was now their corner and even then I seldom called it. But I was among the most conservative.

JIM MAYO

In class students were taught not only the calls but also how to be square dancers. They learned that dancers were friendly people who played in teams. It was fun for the team to succeed but they were also taught that failure was to be expected. They learned that failure - or breakdown of the square - was not a reason for blaming others. It was accepted as part of the fun. If you couldn't learn to be comfortable, or at least not unbearably miserable, in a square that was broken down while other squares around you continued to dance, you probably couldn't be a square dancer.

The effect of this program of indoctrination was to select into the square dance community an extraordinarily compatible group of people. They had to be reasonably intelligent just to master the complexity of the dancing. They also had to be team players who could share both success and failure with their teammates. Callers and dancer leaders were always on the lookout for potential leaders who were encouraged to help with the work of the club. Nearly everyone was recruited to bring dishes to the potluck suppers. Helpers were always needed to fill out squares in the class. Experienced dancers mixed with the class members to make them welcome and help them learn more easily.

Many clubs had club costumes with unique dress designs usually complemented by matching shirts for the men. While it was possible to buy square dance costumes, many women sewed their own. The design of the club costume was sometimes a matter of serious contention. It has been known to provide the basis for a division that led to creation of a new club.

There were several advantages in this encouragement to help with class. The established club members made friends with the new recruits during the class. When they graduated and came to the club events they already had a group of friends. The helper role also made it more comfortable for graduates who weren't fully confident of their dancing skills to effectively repeat the class. In fact it was not unusual for some to dance only with the class because they lacked the confidence to dance with the club.

This activity was not for everyone. Even in the early days no more than a quarter of those who tried it became regular square dancers. Initially, nearly everyone that started class stayed through graduation even as the learning period stretched to more than twenty weeks. After graduation, however, nearly half of the people never came back. Another half of those who finished the season dancing with the club didn't come back when the next season began. In those early days we didn't give too much thought to that defection. We had enough graduates to keep the club growing even when we kept only a quarter of those we taught.

Those who stayed found themselves in an activity that absorbed them. Many clubs met weekly or twice a month on a weekday but that was just the beginning of the dancing experience. In addition to those weekday events that were usually called by a club caller and were sometimes called workshops, clubs sponsored weekend dances. Groups of dancers from a club traveled to these weekend dances together, both those sponsored by their own club and those sponsored by commercial square dance halls and neighboring clubs. And that could be a big neighborhood.

In 1959 Ray Lang invented the Knothead badge. A group of dancers took a bus trip from Seattle, Washington to a dance in Vancouver, British Columbia. The group concluded that they must be "knotheads" to make such a trip. Ray came up with the idea of a badge to recognize such trips. Back at home he designed the badge, a wooden one with a knotted string passing through it. In the next couple of years the word spread and the badge became popular all over the country. It was one of the early entries in a group of badges given in recognition of special square dance activities. The qualification requirements developed by the originating group in Seattle called for a group of at least four couples to travel together to a dance one hundred miles or more from their home. It was a very popular badge. There was another badge called the Rover for couples that traveled 1000 miles to dance but they could do it by themselves.

The Century Club Badge was created in 1960 by a couple of new graduates from the class in Westfield, Massachusetts. To earn it a dancing couple collected one hundred caller signatures in a specially designed autograph book. Each page had a place for the date, the location of the dance and the caller's signature. Only three signatures could be collected on the same date to prevent someone going to a big convention and filling the whole book in one weekend. I know many people who collected their one hundred signatures in their first year with the book. Some of them would go to two and three dances in the same night dancing a single tip at each one, collecting the signature and traveling hastily to the next dance. I also know several couples that have filled two and three books.

Another badge that helped to build the social bonds in the square dance club was the Idiot Badge. For this a group of dancers, at least a square, was required to travel to a caller's home late at night to wake the caller to call a tip for them. It was a popular badge and, often, club members facilitated new graduates' earning of this one by accompanying them to their teacher's house. I had a standing rule that any group coming to my house for an Idiot Badge was expected to come prepared to stay through the night - and bring breakfast with them. Many groups did and I requested steak and eggs for breakfast.

This type of involvement with other square dancers built strong ties. The strength and length of the friendships built in square dance clubs is hard to imagine outside the activity. Many people who met on the first night of class twenty and thirty years ago are still, today, close friends. They are still dancing together if they can but the friendships survive immense challenges. The friendship-building skills they learned in class remain with them even when they retire and move to new areas. If there is a club in the new area, they find a group ready to welcome them. I have often said that square dancing is as good as a church for welcoming newcomers to an area. A couple from one of my clubs who were also active in their church found the square dance club to be as helpful as the church but in a different way when they moved to a retirement location. The church, they said, was a less diverse group than the square dance club. The club included more of a cross section of the community.

# CHAPTER 10 - 1970 - THINGS ARE CHANGING

As modern square dancing headed into the 1970's it was a robust, expanding recreation that seemed to please everyone who tried it. It was never easy to persuade people to come to their first night of square dancing. It looked complicated. Men were seldom comfortable with the idea of dancing - any kind of dancing. To get them through the door that first night of a class was a real project. But this was a generation of joiners. Many wives were still spending their days at home and they were eager for a night out. When friends told them about the fun they were having square dancing, they managed to get their husbands to the class. And that was all it took. During that era, I assured my club members that if they would get the new recruits there one night, I would keep them. It was easy to make good on that promise. Men discovered that this was a different kind of dancing. It didn't take any fancy footwork and it was exciting. You didn't really know what was coming next but the caller tried hard to make sure that you got it right. It was rare, in the late 1960's and early 1970's, for anyone to drop out of a square dance class. If they came through the door, it was almost certain they would complete the class.

Classes were extending far beyond the ten weeks I was using in 1960. In my 1966 caller school, I laid out a twenty-seven week teaching plan that included thirty-eight calls plus another five that might be included if the class was learning well. In the 1972 edition of Jay King's book *How to Teach Modern Square Dancing,* he presented a twenty- week beginner class with thirty-three calls and an additional ten weeks for an intermediate course bringing the total count of calls taught to fifty. The report of Bob Osgood's Gold Ribbon Committee had been published (December 1968 and January

1969), identifying a Basic Program to be taught in ten weeks that included twenty-eight calls [7] and an Extended Program of twenty-four additional calls for which twenty weeks of class were recommended. All of these counts of figures taught are approximate because each author, in numbering the calls, gave numbers to parts of calls or variations of basic actions that makes a direct comparison of the numbers uncertain. One important observation that can be made regarding these three recommendations is that they all agree on a teaching rate of about one-and-one-half calls per class.

Another interesting observation that can be made about all of these lists is that they effectively ignored the rising flood of new calls. As noted in Chapter 7, the 1970 Edition of Bill Burleson's encyclopedia listed 1679 calls. Yet the three lists mentioned differ only by the inclusion of a few calls that were created between 1966 and 1972. Clearly, the impact of new call creation was not being felt in class. Callers were introducing the new calls by teaching them as they used them and the basic movements of square dancing were quite stable. There was a reasonable consensus that it would take about thirty weeks to teach new dancers these basic movements at a rate of about one-and-one-half calls per class.

## THE DANCE EXPERIENCE IS CHANGING

While the entry into modern square dancing was reasonably standardized throughout the country, the experience of dancing after class was changing. New clubs were forming with new callers. Some of these callers had been to a caller school. Many had not. The population of dancers was never counted but must certainly have exceeded a million[8] and could easily have been twice that. The circulation of *Sets in Order* hovered around 20,000 and *American SquareDance* was reaching fewer than that. These magazines and

---

[7] The Gold Ribbon Committee Report numbered nineteen calls and variations of these plus four "glossary" terms into a list of fifty teaching terms. These were widely accepted over the next decade as the Basic Fifty terms of square dancing even though many were variations of a single call. As an example, Right Hand Star, Back by the Left and Star Promenade each received a numbered place in the Basic Fifty list.

[8] In many publications the peak dancer population has been estimated at five million. Bob Osgood once told me that he created that number in response to a call from a national magazine asking him how many square dancers there were. The organization Legacy tried to conduct a census in 1990 and concluded after some statistical manipulation that the total number of club dancers (another way of saying modern, not traditional) in the United States was about 375,000

the note service publications for callers were beginning to bring about a common understanding of how square dancing should be done but there was no real standardization. Each of the traveling callers had his or her own style. Some emphasized smooth dancing that kept the dancers together with a solid musical beat and phrase. Others began to de-emphasize the music in favor of increasingly intricate choreography. The use of new calls by traveling callers at weekend dances was commonplace. Club callers were struggling to keep up with the new calls their dancers were hearing every weekend. My club in Topsfield, Massachusetts met every Monday for "workshop." In the 1970's that term really described the program. I put out a sheet of paper on the table each Monday and invited club members to write the new calls they had encountered since the previous Monday. It was common to find six to eight different calls on that list each week.

The caller/club relationship varied widely. In New England the usual arrangement was that a club danced to their "club caller" on a weekday night two or four times a month. Most clubs then sponsored a "guest" caller on one weekend night once a month. In the early days, when the density of clubs was sparse, this schedule resulted in a minimum of competition at the weekend dances. There were plenty of dancers to go around. In Northern California the number of clubs had grown substantially. The dancers' association there established a system of scheduling guest caller dances to reduce the direct competition among them. Most clubs were permitted to run no more than two or three such dances each season. The effect of this regulation was to increase the number of dancers at each dance. Dances with sixty squares in attendance were common there. In Southern California there were very few "club" callers. Clubs had a single caller as class teacher, but for the weekly dances they hired a different caller each night. This "guest caller" format helped bring more variety to the club dances, but made the class to club transition for the new dancers more difficult. Jon Jones who lives in the Dallas area reports:

> The relationship of caller and club in my area in the early 60's was that nearly all of them were officer or committee run. The caller was hired. They are still that way [with] very few exceptions. However, the caller was considered part of the club. We all referred to them as "my club" and most of us were very involved with the club operations in an advisory capacity. I know I was, as was Melton Luttrell, Ray Smith, Harper Smith, C.O., Guest, Billy Lewis, Joe Lewis and all of the better active callers. If we thought they were headed in the wrong direction, we would advise them as best we could. All clubs had a "club caller." In the Houston area

most clubs did not have a regular club caller. Very few do today. They hire a different caller for each dance. Almost all other areas of the state had a regular caller. That was always a bragging point for most clubs to say "we've got so-and-so as our caller."

One important change that became very evident during the 1960's was a growing divide between the experienced dancers and the new graduates from classes that nearly every club was sponsoring each year. Many dancers, both experienced and novice, didn't go to the traveling caller dances. They got all the dancing they wanted at the weekly or biweekly meetings of their club(s). Their only exposure to new calls was as their club caller taught them. Their interests and program needs were quite different from those dancers who regularly danced to traveling callers. Some callers were not too considerate of the dancers in the way they presented new calls. I remember all too well an incident from my own experience. I had traveled nearly 100 miles across Massachusetts to attend a dance with members of the Merrivales, my club in Haverhill, Massachusetts. One of the guest callers introduced a call I had never heard before with the words, "If your caller's been doing his job you've probably already seen this call but let's walk through it anyway." Needless to say, I was less than pleased. It was that kind of attitude that helped fuel a building tension between the local callers and their traveling counterparts. It also contributed to the divide between the dancers who were happy to dance at their club once a week and those that wanted to know-it-all at the weekend dances.

In addition to the growing number of clubs, there were square dance halls developing in many areas. Some of these were built by the clubs in a community and several clubs danced in this community facility on different nights of the week. Some were built as commercial ventures by callers or dancers. With either sponsorship there was likely to be a traveling caller dance on Saturday night - every Saturday night. At the club dance there was a substantial social pressure to dance with everyone. The experienced dancers were strongly encouraged - even urged - to dance with the recent graduates. In spite of that pressure, the experienced dancers were often not eager to include the new dancers in their squares. When they went out on Saturday night, they were even more reluctant. They wanted to be dancing in the squares that succeeded and that often meant going to the dances in groups of four couples. It was common for the squares at the front of the hall to be made up of the same couples dancing in the same squares and often in the same place on the floor all evening.

All of this, of course, goes against the party line. Square dancing is a wonderful social activity that welcomes everyone. We teach dancers in class that they must not form "cliques." They must mix with other dancers. That has always been the party line. It has, however, been true from the earliest days of square dancing that the better dancers, given their choice, would prefer to dance with each other. I remember my earliest encounters with traditional square dancing in the Monadnock region of New Hampshire in 1947. As I crossed the floor with my partner toward one of the "good" squares it would evaporate before my eyes or another couple would appear seemingly from nowhere to fill the vacant space. Since the program at those dances alternated squares and contras the experienced dancers could check out your swinging skill during the contra. Once I had mastered the fine points of swinging, that experience became much less frequent. In the club setting the tendency for experienced dancers to stay together was under considerable pressure. It was clear to nearly everyone that the dancing for the whole group would improve if the less experienced dancers were distributed among the "old-hands." As a dancer, I hated mixers but as a caller I used them often to balance the dancing skills in the clubs I called for.

## THE CLOSED CLUB AND DANCE DIFFERENTIATION

One manifestation of this eagerness of the experienced dancers to avoid the beginners began to appear in the late 1960's. It was the closed club. These groups were started and managed either by experienced dancers or by callers. Membership was by invitation and it was common to have some form of audition for prospective members. In my own North-of-Boston area there were five such groups and that was typical of other active square dance regions around the country. Many of these groups concentrated on experimenting with new calls that were being written at a rate that assured few clubs could learn even a small share of them. Most experienced dancers had not realized - or perhaps accepted is a better word - that few of these calls would enter the permanent vocabulary. They worried that they would be embarrassed by not knowing a call that a traveling caller used without a walk-thru. They also wanted to dance with others who took their dancing seriously. And there were more than enough experienced dancers to fill these invitational groups.

Under the influence of the training I had received from Ed Gilmore, the invitation-only group that I started, Jim's Gems, was dedicated to using the "standard" calls of that time in a greater-than-usual variety of setups. While I didn't teach any of the new calls in that group, I did take advantage of the considerable dancing experience of the people who were admitted to the group. I also gave more than the usual emphasis to dancing style. I had no trouble maintaining the membership of nine sets that filled the hall we used. We danced every other week and members paid for a series of six weekday dances at a time (whether or not they attended) although few ever missed a dance.

There was also, at this time, a distinction building between dances. More callers were learning to provide variety in their choreography with one or more of the choreography control methods. Increased choreographic variety was one of the important differences between the midweek club dance and the weekend dances called by the visiting callers. In the early 1960's most of the callers who traveled were experienced and skillful. During the 1960's an increasing number of callers discovered that a reasonable living could be made on the road. It was common, during that period for a well-known caller to spend two or three weeks in New England calling at the commercial square dance halls on Saturday nights and for weekday club dances every other day they were in the area. Those among them who taught callers were sometimes hired by caller associations for a clinic on the Sundays. It was hard work but there were lots of clubs and it paid quite well.

By 1970, in most population centers in the United States and Canada, there were many clubs within a reasonable distance of each other. The weekend dances drew customers from a wide area. The size of that area varied from one region to the next, but many dancers traveled, often in groups, for a couple of hours or more to Saturday night dances. The established, experienced callers were being hired much like the traveling callers. In effect, they were "traveling" callers who stayed in their own region rather than traveling throughout the continent. It was somewhere during this time period when the term "national caller" came into use to distinguish the most popular traveling and festival callers from regional callers who were often equally popular. There was a great deal of discussion about the term. Some identified the callers who traveled extensively as "professional" but several of them had full-time jobs outside of square dancing. There were also a growing number of local or regional callers for whom calling was a primary source of income. There is still not a comfortable acceptance of any term to distinguish the several economic and/or competence categories into which callers can be divided.

The calling skill and the programming philosophy differed widely among these callers. Many of the best-known callers felt pressure to provide a "different" dance experience from what the local callers provided. At the same time the attitude of the dancers was becoming an important factor. The dancers who hired callers were, usually, the most experienced dancers in a club. They were the ones most likely to succeed - and enjoy - even when the caller's ability or attitude made the dancing difficult. It sometimes seemed to many of us that the surest way to get hired back at a club was to call so that only the dancers who hired the caller were successful.

Another component of dancer attitude that had a substantial impact on the development of modern square dancing is the seeming willingness of most dancers to accept complete responsibility for their own dancing success. It seemed impossible for any dancers to hold the caller responsible when their square broke down. They always believed the breakdown was because they were not "good enough" to dance to that caller. Dancers were often heard to say "We couldn't dance to him this year but wait until he comes back again. We'll be ready for him." Unfortunately, many callers seemed to agree that any dancer breakdown was because the dancers hadn't learned to dance well enough rather than any responsibility of theirs. In fact, many callers appeared to view the dancer/caller relationship as a competition. One caller was regarded as more "challenging" than another. Dances often appeared to be a contest to see whether the caller could call material the dancers couldn't do. This was not a new phenomenon. I have a tape of a 1958 dance called in Northern California by Bill Castner and John Strong. In it, after calling a series of Rip and Snorts, John called "Any old couple, ah, Allemande Left..."and then added "Well, I got one square." A bit later in the same tip he called, in a box formation, "Dive Thru, Box the Gnat, Face to the Middle and...Allemande Left" after which he added "There, I gotcha that time." Clearly there was acceptance of the competition mode of interaction between the caller and the dancers.

All of these factors contributed to a substantial difference between dances. When the older, established clubs with a high proportion of experienced members hired callers who thought they should test the ability of the dancers, that dance was no place for dancers newly-graduated from a class. There were, however, many callers who didn't call such difficult material. Often this was because they could not. Occasionally a caller was opposed to the "contest" model of square dancing. Dick Leger was known everywhere as a caller to whom a new dancer could be sent with assurance that they would dance successfully all night. It was about 1970 when Dick and I were talking after a meeting of the Narraganset Callers Association in Rhode Island at which I had been the speaker. We were discussing how difficult it was to provide an interesting program and, at the same time, assure that most dancers were successful. Two of the association members who were listening to our conversation finally could take it no longer. One of them broke in and said "I hear what you guys are saying but I'm really only happy when I'm killing them."

Experienced dancers were well aware of the difference between dances. They understood the code. They knew that some callers would give them several new calls at a dance while others used only the common calls in their dance program. They knew which callers "were only happy when they were killing them" and which were dedicated to a high proportion of dancer success. When Ed Gilmore called at one of the area square dance halls it was a very different dance from the one that Les Gotcher called in that same hall. The differences took many forms. Les wasn't much of a singer and usually did one or no singing calls. He also promoted himself as the "Hash Master" and could be counted on to make the dancing quite different and more challenging than that done at most clubs. Les also was an enthusiastic promoter of the use of new calls. Ed Gilmore, on the other hand, was certain to provide a more rhythmic, musical dance experience with a constant concern for dancer success. These two were near the extremes but there were all gradations between and beyond them. Ed also believed that new calls could only bring trouble for square dancing.

In Ohio, where Willard Orlich, a non-caller choreographer, and Lloyd Litman lived, there was a group of callers who were known for an interest in challenging choreography. Ron Schneider, Johnny Davis and Jack Jackson were the most traveled of this group. Experienced dancers were conscious of the differences between callers and between clubs. When they went to a dance they knew what to expect. Less experienced dancers sometimes found themselves in dance situations where they were not prepared. An interesting view of the addition of new calls into the accepted vocabulary can be seen in a categorized list of calls published in the September 1965 *American SquareDance*. Willard Orlich was reviewing the new calls that he had included in his column in that magazine over the previous thirty-five issues. He identified as "Basic and acceptable" the calls Cast Off, Centers In, Circulate, Cloverleaf, Dixie Daisy, Fold, Outsides In/Out, Peel Off, Run and Cross Run, Spin the Top, Swing Thru, Tea Cup Chain, Trade and Wagon Wheel. In his area of Ohio, these had already been accepted. His judgment would be confirmed with the publication of the *Sets in Order* Extended Basics list in January 1969. Only four of those fifteen calls were not included. The four were Dixie Daisy, Peel Off, Tea Cup Chain and Wagon Wheel.

## THE DISAPPEARING WALK-THRU

One of the ways in which the difficulty of dances varied was the amount of "walk-thru" that the caller provided. At the start of the 1960's, nearly every routine that any caller used was completely memorized. The methods of choreographic control that make improvisation possible had not yet been published. It was common practice for the caller to walk the dancers through a routine before starting to call unless it was very common and familiar to most dancers. Callers often worked an unusual singing call routine into the patter of a couple of tips early to be sure the dancers could do it successfully. Over time we learned that we didn't have to walk the whole figure. We could get the dancers to the setup for the tricky part and walk only that part. That ability, however, developed slowly among callers during the 1960's. At the start of the decade most callers had to walk the entire figure in order to show the dancers even a small part of it.

The walk-thru became, during the 1960's, one of the most important distinctions between an easy dance and one that was more difficult. The first overt recognition of this distinction that came to my attention was a series of dances run by Dick Steele in Lexington, Massachusetts and advertised as "No-Walk Thru" dances. Dick had begun advertising some of his dances as "Advanced" in the late 1950's. In 1961 he added the "No-Walk Thru" designation and these dances were known by everyone to be the ultimate challenging dance at the time. This was before the floodgates had opened to the new calls but the call vocabulary was expanding. The difficulty of these dances was not primarily the vocabulary but, instead, was the absence of any advance notice about the choreographic routine. The routines that were called were composed of modules that most experienced dancers had encountered before. But there was no warning of how those modules would be combined or programmed.

In a communication from Cal Campbell he made this observation about the increasing difficulty of square dancing during the transition from traditional to modern:

> My sense is that the real magnitude of difficulty came in the memory response time burden placed on the dancers. Dancers were expected to hear a command and then respond to that command with less and less time between the first command, the expected action and the next command.

This change in the manner of delivering choreography to the dancers would accelerate as callers became more skilled with the several choreographic management techniques. As the decade of the 1970's began, however, it was still common, at least with most local club callers, to walk the dancers through each routine before it was called. One of the interesting motivations for this practice was to allow the caller to remember the figure before he or she called it. Since nearly everything that was called was memorized, both the words of the call and the pattern of the routine, it was a big help to the caller to walk the dancers through before the needle went down on the record. Certainly the walk-thru was essential for the new calls that were a major part of most club programs. As we will see later, the standardization of call lists by CALLERLAB in the mid-1970's brought about a dramatic change in the amount of choreographic advance notice dancers were given.

## WHAT DID THE DANCERS SAY?

I have long been a fan of direct information. When I went to Ed Gilmore's school he urged us all to keep records. I started keeping track of the folks who went through my square dance classes. Through most of the 1960's I was teaching a class for each of the three clubs that I called for on a regular basis. Nearly everyone who came usually completed the course. They started in late September and continued at least once a week until late April. I don't have the specific numbers anymore but the message I got from all that record keeping remains clear in my memory. Of those who completed the class, about half never square danced again. They attended the graduation dance and then disappeared. Of the other half who continued to dance for the rest of the season (in New England most clubs stopped dancing for the summer), half of those did not return to dancing after the summer break. Thus, from each class, we kept as dancers about a quarter of those who graduated. In numerous conversations with other callers at the time, it became quite clear that my experience was not unusual.

In 1972 and 1973 I was given an unusual opportunity. The Yankee Twirlers, a club with a reputation for appealing to the most eager dancers in the area, asked me to teach a "brushup" class. They sent promotional material to couples who had gone through their classes for the past several years but were not dancing regularly with the club. The program was to be a series of six classes to re-teach the standard calls. This effort recruited twenty-five squares of students who paid for the whole series up front. The program was repeated for a second year and the class size dropped to twenty squares. A year after completion of that second year I sent out a questionnaire to one hundred and twenty couples who had attended either or both years. I was interested to know whether the program had been successful in bringing them back into square dancing. I was also curious to know why those who had not returned were not dancing.

From the mailing of one hundred and twenty I received responses from forty-one which, I am told, is a pretty high response rate. Of the forty-one, twenty-eight were still dancing. Thirteen, almost one third, had once again joined the ranks of non-dancers. The reasons they gave for quitting again give us another window through which to view the state of the activity in the early 1970's. Five of the thirteen had quit for physical reasons or relocation. The reasons offered by the rest included that other dancers were too critical, that there was too much material or that their other activities didn't allow them enough time to keep up with square dancing. I also asked what could be done to make square dancing better. Half of those who were no longer dancing said that there should be easier dances. It is interesting to note that even those who were still dancing offered similar suggestions. A third of them suggested easier dances and another strong recommendation from the still-dancing group was for better preparation.

# CHAPTER 11 - THE CALLERLAB ERA BEGINS

Many dancer and caller associations were formed. Some of these were state based. Others were regional. However, no successful nationwide organization existed for either callers or dancers during the 1960's. Both *Sets in Order* and *American SquareDance* magazines had been involved in attempts to establish nationwide dancer organizations. In 1965, a leadership conference was organized by Arvid Olson, publisher of *American SquareDance* magazine and Prof. Arden Johnson at Purdue University. From that conference came the National Square Dance Association. The reasons for formation and the goals were described in the October 1965 issue with these words:

I    To Unite the Square Dance Movement
II   To Promote Square Dancing
III  To Help Local, State, and Regional Callers' and Dancers' Associations Function More Effectively.
IV   To Analyze Material

The Sets in Order American Square Dance Society was established in 1970. Its avowed purpose was the protection, promotion and perpetuation of square dancing[9]. While both of these were, in part, promotional moves for

---

[9] When the Sets in Order American Square Dance Society was formed the name of the magazine was officially changed from *Sets in Order* to *Square Dance*. Old habits and names, however, die hard and throughout its existence it was known by its original name by nearly everyone. The same was true of *The New England Caller* which changed its name to *The Northeast Square Dancer Magazine* on the masthead but never completely in the minds of the dancers or callers.

the magazines, they also represented the hopes of the founders that increased communication and organization would prove a long-term benefit for the activity. In addition to these attempts at national organization, there were a number of regional dancer organizations that, collectively, recruited an even larger share of dancers into membership.

One of the motives for establishment of a dancer organization was the potential for raising money. It seemed in the 1960's that square dancing was already on an explosive growth track. The early founders of dancer organizations may have hoped to be able to draw from that large population of dancers enough money to encourage and promote the growth and still have some left over for profit. While dancers joined their local clubs willingly and even supported state or regional organizations, they have never been eager to extend their support outside the local area. Neither of these national dancers' organizations ever recruited any substantial number of members relative to the overall population of square dancers in the United States.

## LEGACY FORMATION

One organization that was successful was Legacy. It was formed by the publisher/editors of three of the largest square dance periodicals, Bob Osgood of *Square Dance* (*Sets in Order*), Stan Burdick of *American SquareDance* and Charlie Baldwin of *The New England Caller*. They met in New York in 1971 and agreed to work together to establish an organization with representation from as many facets of the activity as they could bring together. The result was the organization they called Legacy. The first meeting, held in Cleveland, Ohio in May of 1973, was attended by more than eighty leaders from twelve interest areas. They addressed a range of topics including Image, Communication, Heritage, Business, Standardization and Ethics. This organization continued in existence until 2002. It sponsored a number of useful projects ranging from leadership training and promotion to a census in 1990 and a series of attitude surveys.

There were plenty of leaders to recruit into a national organization. In the November 1972 issue of *Square Dance* which announced the formation of Legacy there was a listing of the several types of organizations that were to be invited to take part. The article mentioned 249 dancer associations, 138 caller associations, 32 round dance teacher associations, 144 square dance publications, 35 square dance record companies and an unquantified reference to the businesses supporting the activity with clothing and equipment.

## EARLY CALLERLAB MEETINGS

Bob Osgood had believed for many years that a national organization of callers could exercise leadership that would benefit the square dance activity. The first discussion of such an organization took place at a meeting at one of Ed Gilmore's caller schools in Glenwood Springs, Colorado in the early 1960's. Plans were made that led to the leadership conference held at UCLA in 1964. Bob had also started a "Hall of Fame" in his magazine. He had oil portraits painted by Gene Anthony of callers he felt were deserving of recognition for their contributions to square dancing. The portraits were displayed in the dance hall at the magazine's offices in Los Angeles. He then used the portraits as covers for his magazine. By 1970 he had inducted fourteen of the callers he respected most into his hall of fame. Many of the members of this group had also served on the staff of the square dance vacation institutes that Bob ran at the Asilomar conference facility near Monterey California. It was this group that joined him in the initial stages of the formation of CALLERLAB.

In 1981 Bob wrote a "Prologue to the History of CALLERLAB" which provides us with insight into the state of square dancing in 1970 and the attitudes of some of the callers who joined together to start what became the International Association of Square Dance Callers. I quote it here in its entirety with Bob's permission.

> There have been rumors of an all encompassing callers' association since the 40's. Toward the end of World War II, Ed Durlacher, Lloyd Shaw, Ralph Piper, Ralph Page, Herb Greggerson, Jimmy Clossin and perhaps one or two others maintained a correspondence "Round Robin" where one would write a letter to another, then the second would add comments and send the composite on to a third and so on until the collection reached caller number one, who would call off his original notes from the top, add comments at the bottom and start it off to the list again. [We know from Al Brundage's speech presenting the CALLERLAB Milestone Award to Ralph Piper in 1997 that Al, Bascom Lunceford and Floyd Woodhull were also part of that group.]

> How long this letter writing went on is difficult to say, but somewhere along the line the tape recorder was brought into the picture and the procedure continued in voice form...The purpose

of all this written and voice communicating was to pass along thoughts, to argue origins and, in general, in these early years leading up to the contemporary scene, to encourage and inform each other.

During the 1950's, we saw local callers' organizations springing up in many communities and it was these early groups that established the ground rules, created codes of ethics and set up guidelines for standardization. The big problem here was that with perhaps 100 or more callers' associations, there were almost that many different lists of basics plus dozens of opinions on standardization.

At this point, communications were aided substantially when *Sets in Order* magazine with the assistance of more than 200 callers geographically scattered across North America, combined all that was available in existing lists of basic definitions and styling notes and published the first of its basic movement handbooks. Over a period of time and with some changes over the years, these lists became the "point of reference" for square dancing. Not all callers followed them to the letter, but they could point to them as a fixed reference and then make their own minor personal adjustments.

At one time we counted as many as 18 callers' groups who had basic lists of their own—but this wasn't bad when one took a look at the total number of callers' groups in operation and considered the fact that most callers did use the *Sets in Order* lists as a base, altering it slightly to fit their own needs.

Another situation that crept in with the proliferation of basics, was the need for some form of standard identification of the levels of square dancing. We saw the activity go through such labels as low level, high level, fun level, club level, beginner level, intermediate level, advanced level, etc. We recall clubs that had been in operation for more than a year, listing themselves as "experienced clubs" and dancers rating themselves as one year, two year or three year dancers. But, while the system in any specific area could be understood within that community, it could be confusing to others coming to dance from another area.

What was "high level" in one area could be "intermediate" in another or even "low level" in a third. With more and more dancers moving from one area to another and with the advent of

96

such big dances as the National Square Dance Convention, a standard form of identification had to be worked out. One that all could, and hopefully would, respect and adhere to.

There were other concerns coming into the picture. Callers were not working together in many areas. Ethics, among callers in general, were never faced head-on. New dance material flowed into the activity unchecked and at an alarming rate and this fact alone scared away untold hundreds, perhaps thousands, of dancers.

It was because of all of these things that veteran caller/leaders were concerned for the future of square dancing. Something, some form of organization perhaps, was needed where callers could be encouraged to pull together. It had to be something where each one could have a vote in shaping the direction for callers and improving the callers' image. As one dancer so graphically put it "we go to a leadership meeting and about the first question to come to the floor is 'how do we fire our caller?'"

What was not needed was a simple social fraternity and certainly no one wanted a union. Callers who had first gone the route of being dancers, were the logical ones to lead. But, unless callers understood what it meant to lead, the activity could continue to go on aimlessly. How could such an organization come about? Who could form it? Who possessed the credibility to set the guidelines?

In the 1940's, when square dancing just began to emerge, many areas had their own Messiah. Usually this person was a caller who had been in the activity longer than any of the others. He was usually one who shared his knowledge with those who sought him out and who became his apprentices. Dr. Lloyd "Pappy" Shaw had done this on a national basis through the mid 1950's but now he was gone. To be sure, there were others who had been emerging as leaders, but the activity had grown so greatly that a single leader that all could or would follow was no longer feasible.

This was the concern of a number of leaders during the 1960's. One such group held a several day informal conference in Glenwood Springs, Colorado. Some of these same leaders pooled their efforts in establishing two successful on-campus, professional callers' conferences at UCLA. During this time the need for a respected "body of knowledge" increased and gradually an idea

97

began to materialize. If there was not a single leader who could bring all callers together, perhaps there could be a composite - a group of leaders who, by combining forces, could attract a following. This was the breakthrough!

Such a group of leaders did exist. They were the dozen or so members of the Square Dance Hall of Fame. Together they possessed the necessary credibility. This could be the basis for a meaningful callers' organization. This could be the "body of knowledge" that would attract callers from around the world.

By this time it was 1969. We spent the next two years in planning the skeleton of such an affiliation, at that point unnamed. The research resulted in a list of ten points - some of which had come up in the Glenwood Springs meeting and others at the two UCLA caller seminars. These ten would be the first order of business for this group to handle.

In late 1970, the invitations were out to the Hall of Fame members. The announced purpose of the meeting which was to be held at Asilomar and hosted by the American Square Dance Society, was a banquet and three days of informal meetings with the Hall of Famers as guests of *Sets in Order*. The meetings resulted in CALLERLAB. The ten points that were used as the focal point of the meeting became our original plank and the new International Callers Association was formed.

The thirteen callers who were members of the *Sets in Order* Hall of Fame in 1971 were: Lee Helsel, Arnie Kronenberger, Bob Van Antwerp, Marshall Flippo, Bruce Johnson, Frank Lane, Joe Lewis, Bob Page, Dave Taylor, Don Armstrong, Al Brundage, Earl Johnston and Johnny LeClair. Ed Gilmore died in 1971 before he was included in the Hall of Fame group but he was an active participant in the early meetings that led to the formation of CALLERLAB. The first ten callers on that list and Bob Osgood attended the meeting in February of 1971 described in the last paragraph of Osgood's "Prologue." While not all of the nation's leading callers were included in this list they did represent a major share of the most respected modern square dance callers active at the time. Notably missing from the group was Ralph Page who had decided not to embrace the changes that separated the modern form of square dancing from its traditional origins. Another traveling caller with more than enough stature to have been included who is missing from the list is Les Gotcher. Les was not a "joiner" and had not been included in the organizing activities that were being supported and encouraged by Bob Osgood.

The first meeting of this group generated a list of statements that identified the concerns that had brought the group together[10]. A listing of those statements provides additional information about the circumstances of modern square dancing in 1970.

1. Let's Put the Dance Back Into Square Dancing.
2. An Accepted Form of Standardization is Vital to the Growth and Continuation of the Activity.
3. Caller/Teacher Leadership Training is the Responsibility of the Callers and Teachers.
4. Professional Standards for Callers and Teachers Need to be Established and Maintained.
5. Today's Square Dancing is Due for a Re-Appraisal.
6. The Combination of the Various Parts of the Square Dance Activity Should be Encouraged.
7. The Selfish Exploitation of Square Dancing Should Be Vigorously Discouraged.
8. The Over-Organization of Dancer-Leader Groups Can Pose a Problem to the Future Progress of the Activity.
   This ninth statement was not completely identified and endorsed at the first meeting.
9. The Square Dance Activity Should be Evaluated on a Continuing Basis.

Another agreement reached at the first meeting was to get together again with the addition of a few more members to the group. The second meeting was held in early February of 1972 with eleven callers in attendance. The three new members of the group who attended that meeting were Jerry Haag, Jerry Helt and me. The most important outcome at that meeting was a decision to form a continuing organization and to hold a callers' convention. The question of financing and handling the administrative work was discussed. Bob Osgood offered to treat the new organization as a "wing" of the Sets in Order American Square Dance Society. This provided the new organization with a "home" and administrative support.

---

[10] Although the Prologue by Bob Osgood mentions a list of ten items, the final list numbered eight items on which there was general agreement and one additional item for further study.

There was considerable concern among those present that the generous offer by Bob Osgood would present a problem in the perception that others might have of the new organization. There was an undercurrent of feeling among some in the square dance world that Bob was trying to "take over" the activity. Statement number seven of the list accepted at the first meeting was that the "Selfish Exploitation of Square Dancing Should be Vigorously Discouraged." The *Sets in Order* magazine was pervasive among leaders in the activity and many people were already of the opinion that Osgood had too much influence. Membership in the Hall of Fame that was the basis for choosing the founding group was, after all, at his discretion. Bruce Johnson expressed the concern this way "I'm sure that underneath there exists the problem that some may interpret this as an attempt by Bob Osgood to run or control CALLERLAB." My response to that observation was "It's perfectly clear that the quality of the work to be done needs to have someone who can give it that kind of attention. I can't imagine anyone else being able to understand it enough and bring to it the skills necessary to accomplish it any better than Bob."

Another interesting decision made at this 1972 meeting had to do with membership. A continuing problem for CALLERLAB has been the requirement, in place since the formation of the organization, that full "active membership" in the organization was only achieved by attendance at the annual convention. This policy was begun at the 1972 meeting. At that meeting a second list of caller/leaders who would be invited to join was prepared. The new list added another fourteen names. Supplemental meetings were held at Asilomar in the summers and by the end of the winter meeting in 1973 twenty-five of the thirty-nine who had been invited had actually attended one or more of the meetings. Those twenty-five became the first CALLERLAB Board of Governors. They were: Don Armstrong, Al Brundage, Stan Burdick, Marshall Flippo, Cal Golden, C.O. Guest, Jerry Haag, Lee Helsel, Jerry Helt, Bruce Johnson, Earl Johnston, Arnie Kronenberger, Frank Lane, Jack Lasry, Johnny LeClair, Joe Lewis, Melton Luttrell, Jim Mayo, Angus McMorran, Bob Osgood, Bob Page, Vaughn Parrish, Bill Peters, Dave Taylor and Bob Van Antwerp.

One of my personal favorite square dance leadership experiences happened during the 1972 meeting. It suggests the spirit of cooperation that characterized the group at this time. I have recounted earlier a compromise worked out by Pappy Shaw with agreement of Al Brundage and Herb Greggerson that created the call Dos Paso. During the 1972 meeting at Asilomar a similar change of the square dance vocabulary was negotiated. When the call Star Thru had been invented in 1962, Frank Lane became concerned that it would lead to problems with the Star figures that had, by then, become very common[11]. In reaction to his concern he decided not to use that name and instead to call that action by the name Snaparoo. There was also a call that was first introduced as Barge Thru. The action was, from facing lines of four, a ½ Square Thru followed by what we now know as Trade By. In 1969 someone had recognized that the Trade By action was a useful choreographic component and had given the name to that action. The existence of the call Trade By quickly eliminated the use of Barge Thru for most callers but Marshall Flippo had persisted in using it in his programs. At this 1972 meeting, there was considerable discussion of the need for standardization. In the heat of that discussion, Marshall asked Frank Lane when he was going to quit calling Snaparoo. His response was "As soon as you quit calling Barge Thru." Marshall said "Deal!" and they both lived by the agreement thereafter.

The meetings from 1971 to 1973 succeeded in planning the first CALLERLAB Convention which was held in Saint Louis, Missouri in April 1974. The original group of eight statements had been expanded to fifteen with the addition of these seven:

9. We acknowledge the importance of the club caller system.
10. The National Square Dance Convention is missing the boat.
11. What can CALLERLAB do to be of help to caller-leaders in the future?
12. The need for better communications
13. The need for an experimental movements clearinghouse.
14. The need to study the subject of fees for callers.
15. A means of accrediting callers.

The original group of thirty-two were each asked to identify up to five caller-leaders from their own areas. This process established a group of one-hundred-and-thirty additional callers who were invited to attend this first convention. More than two-thirds accepted the invitation and 114 gathered on an April Monday in the St. Louis Airport Marriot Hotel.

---

[11] Subsequent experience has proven him right. Within a couple of years after the addition of Star Thru to the common vocabulary the inclusion of routines using the "Star" actions had declined noticeably. Some of us learned to use the phrasing "Heads make a right hand star" in place of the previously common "Heads star right." That attention to wording detail made it possible to continue using stars but most callers found it easier to drop the star routines completely.

## THE FIRST CONVENTION

I remember that Monday morning very clearly. The twenty-five members of the founding group met on Sunday to complete the final planning for the Convention. We met late into the night and gathered again early on Monday morning. By noon all that we could do was finished and the group set out from our second floor meeting room to descend the stairs into the lobby. Nearly everyone in that group was considered a legend in the square dance activity. All had been calling for twenty years and many had thirty years of experience. With few exceptions, these were superstars. Descending the stairs we entered a lobby filled with callers every bit as experienced and as legendary as we were. It was overwhelming and I doubt that any of us will ever forget it.

Square dancing is a close community. Nearly every caller there had worked a festival or dance with several of the others. It was common practice for callers to host traveling callers from another area in their homes. I expect that every one of us in that group would count at least a dozen of the others as close friends. Nearly everyone who attended would probably have identified twenty-five of the others as the leading callers in the activity and most of those lists would have included at least half of the founding group of twenty-five. This was a high-powered meeting. Usually when callers got together it was at a festival or dance and in the presence of our customers. We were comfortable joking with each other but we were used to putting on a show for the dancers. We rarely got the chance to interact with a group of our peers in private, to discuss our deepest concerns about our business, a business we loved. In our local associations, this group of callers were the leaders to whom the others looked for guidance. Here we were among equals and we had come together aware of problems and hoping for help in solving them.

This was also a gathering of some of the biggest egos in the business. Part of being a standalone performer is confidence. Without at least the appearance of it, you cannot get up in front of a group and tell them what to do, even when the group is as kind and welcoming as square dancers. The only entourage that most of these callers had was a wife. We did our own booking, made our own travel arrangements, and set up our own equipment, which was a good bit heavier then. This was a group used to putting on at least the show of confidence. When callers got together to talk about the problems in square dancing, most comments started with, "In my groups, of course, we've solved this problem. Here's how I do it." One of the most striking differences at this, and many subsequent CALLERLAB

Conventions was the absence of such bragging. This group was in awe of the others present.

Bob Van Antwerp prefaced his opening remarks with some statistics about those present:

> Counting all the registered callers, we can account for approximately 1,695 years of square dance calling experience or 641,250 hours behind that microphone. Our largest representation of callers are in the age bracket from 46 to 50. Second largest is in the 41 to 45 age bracket. Our youngest caller delegate is 19 and our oldest is 66. We have representatives from 33 states and two provinces of Canada. Two of our callers are from exceptionally great distances; one all the way from Australia and one from New Zealand. We are graciously blessed to have approximately 60 wives of our callers with us today.

One statistic that Bob failed to include was that the only woman caller present was Osa Mathews.

The Board of Governors had identified three of the major challenges facing square dancing as the primary focus of this convention. Frank Lane delivered the opening talk for the discussion groups on the first subject, How We Dance. He identified the issues that caused concern with these words:

> At this time let us actually lay out a list of some of the problem areas that lead to poor styling and poor dancing, then we will go back and see what can be done about correcting some of these. (1) Rough Dancing, (2) Poor Timing, (3) Lack of Standardization, (4) Inadequate Teaching, (5) Non-Descriptive and Awkward Movements.

Nearly everyone agreed that inadequate calling skill and training resulted in poor timing and that, in turn, led to rough dancing. There was a consensus that the dancers were running away with the activity and it was time the callers stepped up to the responsibility for teaching and promoting smoothness and accuracy in the dancers' execution of the calls. The matter of standardization focused eventually on the question of "hands up" or "hands down" in Ocean Wave actions.

The first resolution passed (with two opposed and eight abstentions) at the final session was:

In order to reaffirm our belief in good dancing practices in the areas of styling and elimination of rough dancing for the greater enjoyment of all participants in our activity, Be it resolved that: CALLERLAB endorses the principles of dancing execution and styling as documented in The American Square Dance Society's Basic and Extended Basics programs. The particular emphasis of this endorsement is for the hands-up position for Ocean Wave type movements, such as Swing Thru and Spin the Top.

That resolution set off a disagreement that would continue for more than a decade. Discussion about the proper handhold started early in the convention, was mentioned in each session and continued late into the evenings in the halls. I took part in an intense discussion on this topic in the lobby of the hotel at 2:00 a.m. with Jack Lasry, Al Brundage, several callers from Texas and several others. We tried out various combinations of calls using both hands up and forearms to see if a case could be made for one over the other. In the end, as the vote indicated, there was support for the hands-up styling. However, the reservations that were expressed strongly by a few led to an important acknowledgment which was expressed in the forty-three page wrap-up issue of the newsletter, *Direction*, this way:

The point was made that this resolution is not an attempt to force upon any area a way of doing things differently from the way they are now doing them. It is stating that CALLERLAB endorses the particular subject. If you have no problem in your given area, the intent is not to create a problem in your area. By passing this resolution we endorse the hands-up policy. It is the intent of the meeting to take a stand in recommending, but it is not the function of CALLERLAB to enforce.

That final phrase would be discussed many times in the next quarter century.

The next topic was New Movements and, again, everyone recognized the problem. The New England delegation came to the convention with a petition signed by more than forty-one hundred members of the dancers association in the area, the Eastern District Square and Round Dance Association (EDSARDA). The petition asked the Convention to "take the necessary steps to (1) Establish a nationwide list of 75 basics; (2) Establish a list or lists beyond the 75 basics whereby a club can identify itself or a specific dance for the benefit of the dancer. The list or lists to be reviewed periodically. (3) Set up a means of screening new calls for presentation to the square dance movement; (4) Limit the number of calls introduced each month or year." The problem had been building since the early 1960's when the rate of new call introduction and use was perhaps one per month to the mid-1970's when The Burleson Encyclopedia was growing at more than twenty-five calls per month. In the introduction to the publication of the *Sets in Order* Gold Ribbon Report Bob Osgood said:

> In the guise of "challenge," movements bearing non-descriptive titles came forth by the dozens. Occasionally a term would tell the dancers what to do; more often the terms were non-descriptive and completely unrelated to the character of the square dance activity.

> At first the effect on the dancers didn't appear too damaging but when it became necessary for the average dancer to attend two workshops and three dancing evenings a week to "keep up with the new language," the fun ended for many of them.

That was written five years before the first CALLERLAB Convention and nothing had been done in that five years to slow the creation of new terms. The Sets in Order Basic Program and Extended Program, a listing of seventy-five terms that were widely accepted as the entry vocabulary, had set some limits on what should be taught in class. But there was no widely accepted means of separating the good from the bad in the list of more than twenty-five hundred calls that had been created by then.

At the same time, those callers interested in using a larger call vocabulary were beginning to organize. In the mid-1960's, the term "challenge" was used to identify a type of dancing based not only on a larger vocabulary, but also on more intricate and complex uses of the calls. After a very successful series of challenge after-parties[12] at the National Square Dance Convention in 1966, the National Challenge Convention was started in 1968, by Ed Foote in Columbus, Ohio. The gathering of dancers and callers from many areas soon led to recognition of the difficulty in identifying an accepted vocabulary of calls. There was a core set of terms used by everyone but each caller had an additional set of calls that were his or her favorites. Ed

---

[12] The regular programming at National Conventions ends at 11:00 p.m. Dancing continues after that at after-parties set up by special interest groups. These include state and regional organizations, sponsors of other dance festivals and recording companies. In 1966 an after-party featuring this type of dancing was run all three nights of the convention.

Foote led the effort to agree on a standardized vocabulary and the first list of *Challenge Dancing's Basic Calls* was issued in 1973.

In New England a square dance vocabulary identification system was also being developed. Two dancers, Let Keddy and Art Ballard, had devised a method. Under the name "Square Dance Systems," and with the help of callers John Hendron and Norm Poisson, they identified the calls they felt deserved to be included. In 1974, they published the first complete list comprising more than four hundred calls divided into four "Club Levels" and four additional "Challenge Levels."

In 1972, the founders of CALLERLAB had taken a first step toward vocabulary control by endorsing the Sets in Order *Basic and Extended Basic Program Teaching Manual.* This established a starting point for which choreographic terms should be regarded as universal. At their pre-Convention meeting in 1974 the founders were having second thoughts and were concerned that it might be seen as presumptuous of them to take on the job of evaluating and restricting calls. An understandable fear of terminology chaos encouraged the founders to establish a control method. Ultimately they agreed that only a nationwide organization had any hope of creating a nationwide categorization[13].

CALLERLAB has been criticized and blamed for division of the dancer population by establishing separate programs of dancing. Widespread acceptance of those programs quickly erased memory of the situation before they were established. Segmentation of the dancers was well established by the time CALLERLAB was formed. An article published in the January 1975 issue of *31 Squares*, a monthly publication in the mid-state New York/Pennsylvania area makes it quite clear that several programs of dancing were understood before any were established and named by CALLERLAB. The article describes dance levels existing in 1975 this way:

---

[13] At the time we were using the word international and we had representatives from Australia and New Zealand in attendance, but we were too concerned with the problems in North America to dare to think that we might establish a worldwide system.

| | |
|---|---|
| PROGRAMMING AND DANCER PERFORMANCE LEVELS | Denotes special emphasis of club level dance programs and dancer performance. The variety (not speed or repetition) of calls put together in interesting, stimulating and creative sequences of smooth choreography gradually increases with each level. Greater and greater dancer and caller precision is required to maintain a flowing smoothness in figure patterns. |
| CLUB LEVEL DANCING Relaxed: | Includes the 75 basic moves called at a leisurely and enjoyable pace from the normal or standard setups. Primarily for those dancers who enjoy more singing calls or just want to escape the hectic pace of the open floor. Also good for the recent graduate. |
| Regular: | Should be able to handle the 75 basics from all possible setups and dance the currently popular "mainstream" figures from normal setups. Includes approximately 100 figures at any given time. The top 25 are constantly changing to some extent. |
| CLUB PLUS: Intermediate: | Includes approximately 125 basic moves and experimental figures currently in use. Dancers should have a hold on the 125 basics from different position or setups. Should be able to be handled by any dancer with one year (Note: the local association recommends two years) of club level experience and who regularly attends special dances and club workshops. |
| Advanced: | For those who are looking for something a little extra. Level basically for dancers with a firm hold on the 125 basics from most any position, and who are dancing the 100 challenge basics from normal setups. Dancers at this level are not considered CHALLENGE dancers, but rather ADVANCED dancers who enjoy workshop, but do not wish to donate a lot of time to higher level dancing. |
| CHALLENGE | The key to challenge dancing is variety and the number of calls used. It is not repetition, speed or |

| | |
|---|---|
| <u>DANCING</u> | hot hash where the caller merely speeds up the record and expects the dancer to run through the calls. It is not how "challenged" one feels. The beginner class dancer is challenged by a regular club dance. The "challenge" is for the caller to get the dancers through the great amount of material presented. The average challenge dancer knows approximately 250 figures from all possible positions and setups. The advanced or way out limit is 400. There are two major levels of challenge dancing. |
| Regular: | This is the level of a dancer who has taken a challenge basics workshop and is now dancing a challenge dance. Dancers want to use a lot of material and have it put into interesting combinations but their experience is not complete enough to be extended into the more difficult challenge positions. This is the CLUB LEVEL challenge of <u>CHALLENGE DANCING</u>. There is a lot of material called and a lot of success by the dancer. The caller tries to insure the success of the dancer by using directional calling as much as possible to help the dancer through the material. Up to 275 figures may be used at this level. |
| Advanced: | This level is for the experienced challenge dancer who really works at the game and wants to be challenged. The dancers at this level are looking for the latest and greatest and toughest. They usually have a lot of time to devote to challenge dancing as well as great reaction to positions. Some directional calling is used but not to a great extent as the dancers are expected to know most of the calls well. Most dancers at this level work tapes of a variety of challenge callers. They can handle well over 400 calls with many of the calls broken into small fractions. Tape dancing is considered a necessity at this level as the dancers want to be able to handle well all calls used by every challenge caller. There are very few dancers at this level. |

Jack Lasry was appointed to chair the committee preparing the topic of New Movements for presentation to the first convention. It was a hot topic. The discussion of it and the actions taken as a result of that discussion changed the face of modern square dancing. Many have said that the identification of levels (CALLERLAB has tried in vain to call these programs) was a devastating blow to square dancing. They say that most of the troubles we see about us can be blamed on CALLERLAB's establishment of dance programs. Forgotten are the levels already being promoted by Square Dance Systems in New England and the petition from the New England dancers asking that an identification system be established.

Jack used the word mainstream several times during his presentation of the topic:

> The dancer who goes to the mainstream dance on Friday and Saturday nights also wants to feel that he is mainstream. He wants to feel he can go to a big convention in Washington or Philadelphia or San Antone or California and go out on the main floor at the particular festival and feel comfortable. He wants to feel that he can go to a traveling caller big dance with Beryl Main or Jerry Haag and be able to dance everything they call that night because this is what the traveling caller should be doing, calling mainstream.

A year later that word would become the name of the most widespread program of square dancing.

Jack proposed a solution that would become the basis for the structure of modern square dancing from that point forward. His initial statement of it took two paragraphs:

> I propose the following: That CALLERLAB select a cross section of callers who represent coast to coast, border to border to border, and interest levels within the total picture, a committee of callers who are active in the picture and are interested in participating in this committee. The committee would select on a quarterly basis, one or two mainstream experimental ideas. And that CALLERLAB would then put a stamp of approval on one or two, and no more ideas, within a quarterly system.

> We have appealed to the masses in our growth, but growth has to be directed. We have put signs and levels on things. I believe that CALLERLAB, as a project, needs to establish a better defined

plateau of square dance levels and clubs and dancers and callers alike can figure out where their club fits into this framework. They can then say, this is the philosophy of our club and we have banded together enough people who feel this way and we'd like you to call a dance for us.

This resolution on New Movements passed with none opposed and two abstentions:

In recognition of the problems which result from an unrestricted flow of suggested new terms for square dance use and in an attempt to provide strong support for callers who wish to exercise good judgment in their introduction of new terminology in their local programs, Be it resolved that: CALLERLAB encourage in every way possible development of definitions of dancing levels or plateaus as a basis for clubs to identify their programs. CALLERLAB shall establish a committee of experienced club callers who also have workshop groups that meet regularly to select from proposed workshop material no more than two workshop terms for each quarter of the year. These terms shall be those considered most likely to gain general acceptance over time. CALLERLAB shall encourage all callers to refrain from calling or workshopping any "non-mainstream" terms except those selected as the quarterly workshop terms at a dance event unless that dance be designated a workshop or advanced level plateau.

Thus was the "Quarterly Selections" program established.

The third major topic for this Convention was Caller Accreditation. Bill Peters made the initial presentation identifying two sides to the question. First was uncertainty about what, exactly, is a square dance caller:

We have never sat down and formally agreed on exactly what is a caller. Does a caller have to be able to call contras to lay claim to the title? Does a caller have to be able to conduct a challenge level program in order to be a caller? Does he have to do one-night stands or does he have to round dance? What is a caller? We need to establish in our minds and for the movement generally exactly what a caller is. We must identify the skills, all of them, in which a caller must become proficient.

Which poses the second problem? We have never identified what are the acceptable minimum levels of performance we are going to assign to those skills in order to grant someone the right to call himself a caller...We could argue all night. It needs to be done, however. We have to agree on some standard, acceptable level of the individual's performance.

Caller performance was one aspect of accreditation. The other was accreditation of those who would teach callers. Bill introduced it this way:

We really have no standards now to identify who is competent and who is qualified to teach callers. What are the standards for a guy who hangs out his shingle and says "I'm going to teach callers?" What qualifications must he subscribe to? All too often right now, we have the situation where the blind, unfortunately, are leading the blind. I think this is the kind of problem that has brought about the intense interest in the needed accreditation program.

This final resolution carried with a unanimous vote.

In order to encourage the maximum possible professionalism in the practice of calling for square dancing, Be it resolved that: CALLERLAB shall create an Advisory board to implement an international accreditation program in these following stages: (1) Establish standards for callers' schools in the areas of curriculum, staff qualifications, and teaching methods. (2) Develop procedures for assuring the compliance of present and future callers' schools with such standards as a requirement for accreditation by CALLERLAB. (3) Investigate ways of extending the principle of accreditation to both local caller-coaches and individual callers.

## THE FIRST YEAR

The resolutions on dancing quality, new movements and caller accreditation passed by the 1974 Convention were the only actions of the full group, but there was a substantial body of continuing work that had been started by the founding group. By the end of the first CALLERLAB Convention there were fourteen standing committees. Everyone attending the Convention was assigned to a committee for the year ahead. The committee names show which aspects of square dancing were deemed most significant by the leading callers of the day. They were:

Communications with the World

National Convention Liaison
Round Dancing in the Square Dance Field
Liaison with Area Callers' Groups
Membership
Canada/U.S. Cultural Exchange for Callers
A Benefits Program for Callers
A Caller's Letter of Agreement/Contract
The Basics as a Point of Reference
A Record Tune Clearing House
Halls for Square Dancing
New Dancers
CALLERLAB Liaison with Legacy
Code of Ethics

One of these committees took on new significance as a result of the resolution on New Movements. The founding group recognized the need to establish levels or plateaus of square dancing. Passage of the New Movements resolution started a review of the calls in the *Sets in Order* Basic and Extended Basic lists to determine whether they still included the correct calls.

*Sets in Order* had published and distributed more than 14,000 caller/teacher manuals based on the content of the Gold Ribbon Committee report. Bob Osgood was understandably concerned that revision of the calls on a basic list by a CALLERLAB committee would make these manuals obsolete. Others were concerned that any attempt by this group to control square dancing would not be accepted by the vast majority who were not part of the group. The minutes of the pre-Convention meeting quote my comments when this question was raised:

> I think you have put your finger on a problem that is going to recur throughout this Convention and throughout the life of CALLERLAB and maybe we ought to look seriously at the principle. It has become increasingly evident that we have a group of individuals who are square dance callers and they are going to react negatively to any attempt to control. I think the chances that we will be able to enforce something with this association are pretty skinny and we ought to think seriously about starting out by stressing that this is an information sharing process and not an attempt to control. It is going to have to be that way through whatever we do.

The review committee, with Johnnie LeClair as chair, set to work to establish the list that Jack Lasry had identified as mainstream. It was accepted a year later for a one-year trial. At the 1976 Convention, the Mainstream list was approved as the first dance program to be identified by the new organization. It included sixty-eight calls in three groups. Those calls were:

## BASIC PROGRAM

1. Circle Left & Right
2. Forward & Back
3. Do Sa Do
4. Swing
5. Promenade Family
   (Full, ½, 3/4)
   a. Couples
   b. Single file
   c. *Wrong Way*
6. Allemande Left/Arm Turns
7. Grand Right & Left/Weave
8. Pass Thru
9. "U" Turn Back
10. Split the Couple/Ring
    (Around one, two)
11. Couples Separate/Divide
12. Courtesy turn
13. Chain Family
    a. Two Ladies
    b. Four Ladies
    c. 3/4 Chain
14. Do Paso
15. Right & Left Thru
16. Star Family (2 - 8)
    a. Right & Left Hand
17. Star Promenade
18. Inside Out - Outside In
19. Couples Lead Right/*Left*
20. Circle to a Line
21. Bend the Line
22. All Around the Left Hand Lady
23. See Saw (Taw)
24. Grand Square
25. Box the Gnat/Swat the Flea
26. Square Thru Family
    (Full, ½, 3/4)
    a. Standard
    b. *Left*
    c. *Mixed Sex & Same Sex*
27. California Twirl
28. Dive Thru
29. Cross Trail Thru
30. Couples Wheel Around
31. Single File Turnback
32. Allemande Thar/*Wrong Way Thar*
33. Shoot That Star
    (½, 3/4, Full)
34. Slip the Clutch
35. Half Sashay Family
    a. Standard
    b. Roll Away
    c. *Ladies In Men Sashay*
36. Alamo Style/Balance
37. Star Thru
38. Couples Backtrack

## EXTENDED BASIC PROGRAM

39. Turn Thru
40. Pass to the Center
41. Eight Chain Thru (1 - 8)
42. Ocean Wave Balance (R/L)
43. Swing Thru Family
    a. Right  b. *Left*
    c. *Alamo*
44. Flutterwheel/*Reverse*
45. Sweep a Quarter
46. Veer Left/Right
47. Run Family
    a. Boys    d. Centers
    b. Girls   e. *Cross*
    c. Ends

48. Trade Family
    a. Boys    d. Centers
    b. Girls   e. Couples
    c. Ends    f. Partner
49. Circulate Family
    a. Boys    f. Couples
    b. Girls   g. *Box*
    c. All 8   h. *Single File*
    d. Ends    i. *Split*
    e. Centers
50. Spin the Top
51. Trade By
52. Zoom
53. Wheel & Deal
54. Double Pass Thru

## MAINSTREAM PROGRAM

55. Centers In/Out
56. Cast Family
    a. Off    c. Right
    b. In     d. Left
57. Cloverleaf
58. Slide Thru
59. Fold Family
    a. Boys    d. Centers
    b. Girls   e. *Cross*
60. Dixie Style

61. Spin Chain Thru
62. Peel Off
63. Tag Family (Full. ½)
    a. Line    b. Partner
64. Curlique
65. Walk & Dodge
66. Scootback
67. Fan the top
68. Hinge Family
    a. Couples
    b. Single Hinge
    c. Partner

---

Substitute was added to Zoom in number 52 and Recycle from waves only was added to the list the next year.

Work of another committee that was started before the 1974 Convention was given new significance by the resolution on Accreditation. A first step toward establishing criteria for accreditation of caller schools was determining what subjects should be included in a caller school curriculum. Leaders of several recognized caller schools were available in New England and we gathered for a meeting near Hartford, Connecticut in May 1972. Those present were: Al Brundage, Earl Johnston, Cal Golden, Frank Lane,

Dick Leger and me. We realized that some frequently-used terms of square dancing had not, to our knowledge, been accurately defined previously. We hoped that an agreed upon definition would help to improve communication between callers and between callers and dancers.

The report of that meeting listed nine areas of major importance, generally in order of importance. Each of the major areas was subdivided to indicate their primary elements. The outline of topics included definitions of several terms. Agreeing on these definitions was surprisingly difficult and that made us realize how important it was that the definitions be accepted and understood. The curriculum that came from that meeting was reported to the first convention by Al Brundage. The Accreditation Committee was charged with completion of that work and with investigation of "ways to extend the principle of accreditation to both local caller-coaches and to individual callers" as called for in the Convention resolution.

# CHAPTER 12 - 1974 - 1980 A PERIOD OF RAPID CHANGE

The first CALLERLAB Convention set in motion a groundswell of change. It was not only the result of actions taken by the new organization. Legacy was trying to bring about cooperation among several branches of the activity. ROUNDALAB was formed soon after CALLERLAB to provide the same kind of organization for the round dance teachers. Local dancer and caller organizations, which often published newsletters, were improving communication and cooperation between dancers and leaders. The popularity of this great community-building recreation continued to explode. 1976 was the Bicentennial year for the United States and new attention was focused on our nation's heritage. Square dancing fit well into this picture. The attendance at the National Square Dance Convention, held that year in Anaheim, CA, was 10,000 more than any year before - or since.

An important accomplishment during the first few years of CALLERLAB was a major step toward restricting the flood of new calls. Another accomplishment of equal importance was the agreement by this group of very influential callers on a list of calls that new dancers should be taught. That agreement, which created the Mainstream dance program, promptly began to have an effect. Where the *Sets in Order* list of Basic and Extended Basic calls had won some support, the continued widespread use of new calls by the most respected callers had diminished its impact. The callers who shared in the decisions on a Mainstream list started to use it and to talk about it with other callers. Most dancers also wanted some restraint on the new call vocabulary and acceptance of the list began to spread. In fact, it was pressure from dancers that ultimately established full acceptance of a standard list of calls.

Callers had real reservations about the limits imposed by the new list. They had previously been successful by introducing new calls to the dancing public at most dances. They believed that their customers wanted those new calls in spite of the petition they had received from the New England dancers. While they recognized the situation was out of control, they were unwilling to take any action that would end the introduction of new calls. This was, after all, a folk activity and it was clearly in a period of rapid change. A substantial number of new calls had won acceptance by the whole of modern square dancing. Twenty of the calls on the first Mainstream list had come into common use in the previous ten years.

## EXPERIMENTAL CALLS

To keep a path open for the introduction of new calls while still stemming the flow, the Quarterly Selection program to provide managed trials of new calls had been established at the first Convention. The selected calls were chosen by a committee of callers who worked regularly with workshop groups where they could try a wider selection of new calls in order to identify those with the most promise. The 1976 Convention confronted the question of what to do with these calls as the list grew. The solution was to ask those attending the convention each year to select no more than ten calls to be continued in use for the following year in Mainstream groups as "Experimental" calls. The procedure also provided that any call that stayed on the experimental list for three years would be recommended to the Mainstream Committee for addition to the Mainstream list.

## THE PLUS PROGRAM

In addition to the Mainstream list of calls, CALLERLAB also identified an extended list for use by the more dedicated or eager dancers. It was established first in 1976 as a program of fifteen additional calls and incorporated calls accepted that year as Mainstream Experimentals. This program also introduced the concept of All Position Dancing (APD). The resolution passed at that convention said:

That CALLERLAB endorse(s) a program of dancing beyond the Mainstream Program for a trial period of one year based on the program defined and identified as follows:
Mainstream Plus - Standard Positions

Mainstream Plus - All Position Dancing

Mainstream Plus and Mainstream Plus All Position Dancing embodies the following:

| | |
|---|---|
| Clover Flow | Spin Chain the Gears |
| Dixie Grand | Split Circulate |
| Grand Parade | Tea Cup Chain |
| Pair Off | Turn and Left Thru |
| Outsides in and out | Substitute |
| Peel the Top | Tripe Scoot |
| Red Hot, Ice Cold | Triple Trade |
| Single Circle to a Wave | Anything and Roll |

In addition, the six Mainstream Experimental calls accepted that year were included. They were:

| | |
|---|---|
| Coordinate | Ferris Wheel |
| Half Tag, Trade and Roll | Pass the Ocean |
| Recycle (Waves only) | Chase Right |

By the 1977 Convention the popularity of the new program was well established and it was accepted on a permanent basis with little change from the initial list of calls. There was, however, a continuing flow of new calls that were achieving more than a little popularity. To provide for those calls, a second program was voted. These votes established the Mainstream Plus One and Mainstream Plus Two programs with twelve calls on each. The motions establishing these programs made no mention of the All Position use of the calls. The program sheets that were published did say in connection with the Plus programs that the standard positions should be taught first and that as more positions were taught the terminology should be changed to All Position Dancing.

Three plateaus of dancing beyond the Mainstream and Plus programs were recognized at this convention. They were: Advanced, Basic Challenge and Extended Challenge. Callers working with these programs had established their own list of calls and CALLERLAB agreed to let them continue to manage their own lists. The use of the word "challenge" to identify a segment of modern square dancing appears to have begun in the mid-

1960's. There were a few callers and a few dancers who wanted to extend their involvement and expand their vocabulary of calls. Among the earliest callers to offer this type of dancing were Holman Hudspeth of Michigan, George Campbell from Miami, Lee Kopman and Paul Hunt from Long Island and Deuce Williams in the Detroit area. Lee Kopman was to become one of the most prolific creators of new calls.

As the trickle of new calls grew into a flood, the number of dancers and callers interested in using an expanded vocabulary and more intricate and complex dance patterns grew. Where there were interested and capable callers, they taught dancers and started groups. Where no caller was interested, dancers started their own groups dancing to tapes. To help these people learn the calls some of the callers produced teaching tapes. Jack Lasry and Lee Kopman were among the first to make and sell teaching tapes in 1969/70 and they were followed within a couple of years by Keith Gulley. The ability to experience more complex dancing without the need to have access to a caller resulted in rapid growth of interest in this more challenging type of dancing. The metropolitan areas around Miami, New York, Washington, Pittsburgh, Detroit and Chicago were home to many Advanced and Challenge clubs.

The National Challenge Convention began in 1968 and by 1974 the program had become well enough established to allow the first publication of a list of *Challenge Dancing's Basic Calls*. Almost immediately there was interest in some level of dancing between the then common "club level" and the full Challenge program. The word "advanced" had been developing as an accepted name for this dance program which was based on a subset of the Challenge vocabulary. The first listing of calls in the Advanced program of square dancing was also published in 1974. The building blocks had been developing over a period of years. During the six-year period from 1974 to 1980 all the major programs of dancing that we knew as we entered the new millennium twenty years later had been identified, named and accepted.

## ACCREDITATION

Another important action taken by CALLERLAB in its early years was the establishment of accreditation procedures. The 1976 Convention accepted a program of accreditation for callers and made it a requirement that all members achieve that accreditation within two years. The program required that a caller must have been an active caller for at least three years. Active calling was defined as calling an average of once per week. The program was based on a point system that recognized both experience and training but was structured so that qualification required a minimum of three years of "active" calling. A second accreditation action taken was the establishment of Caller Coach accreditation procedures. Initially, accreditation was based entirely on experience. To qualify, a coach had to have been actively calling for ten years and have taught "five caller training programs encompassing the full Caller Training Curriculum" that had been approved the year before.

The Accreditation Committee recognized that experience alone was not an adequate basis for qualification as an accredited coach. Even as the procedure was approved the committee was at work developing a written test. The process of test development was a challenge. Eighteen callers[14] were recognized as the most active in teaching callers. They were each asked to contribute questions with their own answers. The full set of about 250 questions was compiled into a written test which was then sent, without the answers, to each of those taking part in the process. The completed tests were compared to provide a consensus set of correct answers. For many of the questions the correct response was clear. For many others, however, there was no agreement on what the correct answer should be. At the 1978 Convention most of the teachers involved sat together to review the results. When they could agree on one correct answer, that question was kept for the final scoring. When there was not agreement, the question was removed. The remaining set of nearly 200 questions was then used to score the tests taken previously by these teachers. That set of questions also became the basis for the written tests administered to future candidates.

The procedure for Coach Accreditation was also modified in 1978 to provide for an oral examination by two other Accredited Coaches after the written test had been passed. The original group of coaches wanted to avoid

---

[14] The eighteen callers were: Bill Peters, Frank Lane, Jim Mayo, Earl Johnston, Al Brundage, Dick Jones, Johnny Davis, Vaughn Parrish, Cal Golden, Jack Lasry, Stan Burdick, Ron Schneider, Bill Davis, Lee Kopman, Lee Helsel, Bob Van Antwerp, Harold Bausch and Dave Taylor.

the perception that they had voted themselves accreditation without having to meet the standards they were establishing for others. The group agreed that they would follow the same procedure. They required that each of the original group achieve a passing score (90%) on the full set of approved questions based on their responses before the approved questions had been identified. They also required that initial accreditation be granted only after an oral examination by two others in the group. To meet this requirement, I flew to Florida where I spent two full days with Jack Lasry and Al Brundage while we each examined the qualifications of the other two. Since we had worked together on several schools, we already knew the areas of knowledge - and weakness - in the others. In our group, at least, we examined with considerable intensity. A similar process was undergone by each of the others in the initial group of Accredited Caller Coaches. (The title was originally Caller Education Specialist but was changed to Caller Coach the next year.)

The Accreditation Committee also knew that there had been a problem in trying to identify the qualities required in a caller accreditation program. In a report to the 1976 Convention, Bill Peters, as chairman of that committee said:

> First of all, when we first considered the question of caller accreditation, just about everyone on our committee – myself included – approached it with the idea of trying to develop a simple performance-type test – a sort of CPA examination that would allow us to separate those who were qualified from those who were not. And I am also sure that we all felt, at the beginning at least, that [it] shouldn't be an especially difficult thing for us to do. The idea was to first decide on exactly what a caller is - what skills must he be proficient in - and then to develop an impartial and a totally objective way of measuring an applicant's ability to perform those skills and to exercise those techniques. And I guess when you say it like that, it DOES sound like it ought to be a fairly simple thing to do.

> But of course you and I both know that simply isn't so…I for one found that in many cases the real skills of a square dance caller were very elusive and very hard to pin down. I found them to be extremely delicate and sensitive because they were based, in large measure, upon the careful exercise of each caller's own personal and highly individual judgment…and such skills have always been extremely difficult to define.

The subject is further complicated by the fact that even in situations where you could define and measure this or that calling skill, you immediately became aware of one or more callers who were quite successful, despite the fact that they lacked a degree of proficiency in a certain calling skill or technique...And what this said to me was that any effective system of caller accreditation would have to accommodate not only those who were successful because they COULD meet our requirements, but also those who were successful even though they could not!

The Accreditation Committee called for establishment of a "standards committee" charged with the responsibility of investigating and defining minimum standards of acceptable performance in the skills and techniques of calling square dances. That committee was established by the Board of Governors with Herb Egender as chairman. The outcome of this effort confirmed what the committee had concluded.

In a report to the CALLERLAB Board of Governors a year later Herb reported as follows:

After consulting with many callers and much research a list was established of what a caller should be. It fell into two categories.

(1) Personal Attributes
(2) Calling skills and techniques

A questionnaire was then distributed asking how important these things were. We tried to score objectively each area and then it was sent to members of the committee for feedback. Their answers ran the gamut. I (Herb) have prepared a CALLERLAB guidance letter which will be discussed in the open meeting (at the 1978 CALLERLAB Convention) on Tuesday. The results indicate that although everyone would like to have an objective list of do's and don'ts, it is just not possible. The best we can do is to come up with a guidance letter which we can give to the callers and (which) could perhaps be used in accreditation. The end result looks very much like a code of ethics.

The discussion during the Convention effectively confirmed what the committee had learned. For every attribute or skill that someone felt was essential for good calling it was possible to find at least one and usually several recognized and successful callers who lacked that skill or attribute. This realization confirmed in the minds of many the basic philosophy of the accreditation process that had been adopted two years earlier. The only measure of calling adequacy is the vote of the dancers. If a caller calls fifty or more dances a year (presumably with dancers in attendance) then he or she may be considered proficient.

## DEFINITIONS

One of the most far reaching projects undertaken by the new organization of callers was the creation of a set of definitions for the calls in common use. *Sets in Order* published the work of the Gold Ribbon Committee in December 1968. In early 1969 the magazine published *The CALLER TEACHER Manual* including definitions for each of the calls on the Basic Fifty list. This was supplemented soon after with a manual for the Extended Basic Twenty-five. These manuals provided definitions for each of the calls and also offered advice on how many steps the dancers should take in executing each of the actions. They also included suggestions for how the actions should be styled. These were the manuals endorsed by the founding group of CALLERLAB at their 1972 meeting.

The first issue of Bill Burleson's *The Square Dancing Encyclopedia* came out in 1970 and included descriptions of all of the calls then in common use. In most cases these were similar to the descriptions provided in the *Sets in Order* manuals but only rarely were they exactly the same. Other publications provided variations from these descriptions also and none of them were truly designed as definitions. Furthermore, many callers made no reference to a definition in teaching a call. They merely taught it to their students as they had first learned it when they started square dancing. As long as the use of the call was from the usual setups these slight variations in description caused little trouble. However, as callers started to explore ways to provide variety without introducing new calls they began to stretch the ways in which they used the calls on the Mainstream list.

By the 1977 Convention, a small committee had succeeded in producing a set of standard definitions for the first thirty-eight calls on the Mainstream list. The objective of this effort was to use consistent terminology and format throughout. Their first effort was accepted for a one year trial period at that convention. Standardized definitions for the remainder of the sixty-eight calls then on the Mainstream list were accepted for a similar trial in 1978 and by 1979 a full set of definitions had been accepted. They were widely distributed by CALLERLAB but work continued as wider use of the definitions continued to turn up problems.

Two other committees had been working in related areas. The Styling Committee with Melton Luttrel as chairman was following up on the initial discussion of hand position that began at the first convention. They worked through the list of calls describing in detail a recommendation for hand hold, facing direction, turning direction and even skirt action for the ladies when appropriate. Reaching a consensus on these matters was only slightly less contentious than had been the initial discussion of ocean wave hand hold. They were able, however, to agree and win a supporting vote for their work.

The other committee involved in the detailed characterization of the Mainstream calls was the Timing Committee. Under the chairmanship of Dick Leger, this committee spent a significant time at each convention actually dancing each of the calls in different sequences and setups with committee members counting the actual number of steps the dancers took in the execution of the actions. In the course of this experimentation the committee had recognized for the first time that the number of steps required for completion of an action changed when the setup changed. This realization had been intuitive on the part of some callers but this committee's work made clear to everyone that a Right and Left Thru done by the Heads in a square formation took eight steps but when done by two couples from a box formation it took only six. By the 1980 Convention, this work had nearly been completed for all the calls on the Mainstream list. A supplement to the CALLERLAB newsletter *Direction* in June 1980 included a complete list of definitions with timing and styling recommendations. An accompanying note pointed out that this was the thirteenth draft of the definitions.

# CHAPTER 13 - SQUARE DANCING IS EVERYWHERE

As we entered the 1980's, it certainly appeared that modern square dancing was destined to grow without limits. People who had learned to square dance in the previous twenty years now filled clubs in every region of North America. Many larger cities had several clubs and even in the populated rural areas hardly anyone was more than twenty miles from a square dance club. The only true, broad measure of the number of participants in any phase of square dancing over the last fifty years is the attendance at the National Square Dance Convention. We have actual attendance numbers from the first one in 1952. With the exception of the extraordinary spike in 1976 there was a fairly steady growth from the beginning of just over three thousand to a peak of almost 31,000 in 1983.

There is no assurance that this one "firm" statistic indicates with any accuracy the size of the general population of square dancers but it is all we have. It probably provides a reasonable indication of the rate of change in the dancer population. The number fluctuates with the location of the convention each year and we can't even be sure that the number was derived by the same method each year. Some cities have "beaten the average" more than once. Louisville, Kentucky, Memphis, Tennessee and Anaheim California have each had much better attendance than the conventions on either side of theirs and they have each done it two times.

## LEGACY CENSUS

Legacy, the organization formed to represent several components of the activity, carried out a number of surveys of square dancers during the

1980's. In 1990 they attempted to do a census. The process was based on the *National Square Dance Directory* which has been published annually since 1978 by Gordon Goss in Brandon, Missouri. Many have questioned whether this directory is a realistic basis for such a survey but, again, it is all we have[15]. That 1990 survey estimated that there was a total of 375,000 dancers in the United States. This is a long way from the five million that had been accepted for many years as a benchmark number by leaders in the activity. The Legacy survey, however, focused exclusively on club dancers. It was based on a directory of square dance clubs. The five million estimate probably originated with Bob Osgood who was certainly including in his estimate people who had danced in school or at community parties or in traditional groups that were not represented in the National Directory.

Whatever the actual number of dancers, it is clear that in 1980 modern square dancing had been a very popular and rapidly growing social recreation for the previous two decades. Throughout most of the 1970's any group that offered square dance lessons in any reasonable population center could count on at least five squares signing up for the course - and the course was once a week for twenty to thirty weeks. It is also clear that the Legacy estimate was a snapshot of the active dancer population at the time of the survey. We know that for every dancer who became a club member at least three others went through class. We have also tried, from time to time, to estimate the average dancing life of those who become club members. The estimates range from three to five years although many who learn become life-long participants. In my own judgement I have extrapolated from the few numbers we know to estimate that today there are well over ten million people who have experienced modern square dancing at least through completion of a class.

## OVERSEAS GROWTH

In the 1980's, modern square dancing was also growing vigorously in many overseas areas. In Germany the activity had been introduced by United States military personnel in the early 1960's. In 1976 when I visited the Heidelberg area there were not many callers who were German nationals. There was a substantial debate underway within the European Callers and

---

[15] The Legacy survey indicated a listing of 287 clubs in New England. The New England Directory listed 183 clubs all of which had to belong to EDSARDA. A dancer survey I conducted that year received responses from 145 clubs. I have long felt that I had information from about half of the dances being held and this is consistent with the Legacy sample information.

Teachers Association (ECTA) over the wisdom of teaching in German. Most clubs included Americans. By the end of the 1980's there were many German callers thanks in large part to the caller training programs that were being run by Al Stevens who had decided to stay there after his discharge from the U.S. Air Force. Many classes were being taught in German and there were many clubs that included only German nationals. That same progression had taken place in England, although the teaching language was not an issue there. Perhaps because the language was less of a problem there, local callers were quicker to start their own clubs independent of the participation of Americans.

American square dancing was introduced to Scandinavia in the 1980's by telephone and oil workers who had encountered it in the Middle Eastern oil fields. It had been introduced there by American oil field workers. The activity was received enthusiastically, particularly in Sweden. American callers were brought over to Sweden in increasing numbers throughout the 1980's to call for festivals and to teach local callers. When I went to Ronneby, Sweden in 1986 I encountered, for the first time, a style of festival programming that is still common and unique to that area. Every other tip was limited to the CALLERLAB Basic program of calls which at that time included the first forty-nine on the Mainstream list. The intervening tips alternated between Mainstream and Plus. I was told of this plan when I was hired and I was also assured that the dancers would be very competent with any setup in which I chose to use the calls. I was furnished with tapes of local callers to validate this information and my calling friends who had been there assured me that it was all true. No amount of warning, however, prepared me adequately for the pace of the program. Between Friday evening at 7:00 p.m. and Sunday afternoon at 2:30 p.m. I called sixty-six tips. There was no round dancing and the breaks between tips were nonexistent. As fast as I could change records the squares had reformed on the floor. I was provided with a backup caller to fill in for me in the event nature called so that the dancing wouldn't be interrupted. That caller also did a full hour of the program each afternoon. It was true that the dancers were much more skilled with complicated uses of the calls than any dancers I had encountered before - or since. I will never forget my investigation of this ability with a sequence that set up a left-handed ocean wave and then alternated Circulates and Split Circulates. There was no sign of difficulty on the floor at all and at home there would have been no squares that succeeded with such a combination.

Early issues of *Sets in Order* include mention of square dancing and a callers' association in Wellington, New Zealand. That early activity had waned some and a vigorous revival and introduction of the modern form was begun by Art Shepard, a Canadian who moved to Christchurch in 1965 after retiring from the Canadian Air Force. Language was not a problem and by 1980 there were well-established clubs in the North Island in addition to the very dominant club in Christchurch run by Shepard. I first visited New Zealand in 1981 at the invitation of Art Shepard who arranged for me to call at a weekend festival in Auckland and another in Christchurch. The technical skills of the dancers there were not very different from those of the dancers in my own clubs but the dancing style was outstanding. The dancers showed little interest in complicated choreography and moved with a style and grace that had virtually disappeared at home. In each city, in addition to the dances I called, I conducted a clinic for the local callers. There, too, I found less interest in intricate choreography than was common at home. I had a reputation for knowledge about the use of the voice in calling and that was a topic of great interest for the callers. One other subject that proved to be of great concern for the callers was the price of admission. Art's club maintained an admission charge of $1.25 per person that was just over half that amount in American dollars at the time. Both calling equipment and records were priced in American currency and were prohibitively expensive for New Zealand callers. They had been trying to persuade Art to increase the admission at his club so they could earn enough money with their smaller groups to afford the equipment they needed. Art resisted on the grounds that his very large club would make (for him) an embarrassingly large income. It was also clear that his pricing policy prevented the rapid growth of competition.

In Australia, square dancing had been introduced in the early 1950's by Joe Lewis who was from Texas. It spread quickly, aided by the promotion of the David Jones chain of fashion stores. The boom faded but square dancing was established and continued in clubs across the country. In the mid-1980's, Bill Peters and I spent a month there conducting a week-long school for callers in Sydney, Melbourne, Adelaide and Perth. In each school there were a dozen or more callers and the dances we called drew twenty squares or more. The style of the dancing there was not very different from that in our own clubs back home but the program was exclusively Mainstream. At that time there was little interest in the Plus program anywhere that we went in Australia. One thing that was different was the tempo of the dancing. By that time, the 132 beats per minute (bpm) that had been a minimum during much of the 1960's in America had become a maximum. Both Bill and I were calling at a tempo of 126 bpm because we had found that the dancing became ragged when we went much faster than that. The Australians were still calling at 132 bpm or more and they insisted, when we tried to slow them down, that their dancers demanded that tempo. At the same time, their dancers were asking us if we couldn't persuade their callers to slow down and call more like we did. When I went back for the Australian National Convention and the Australian CALLERLAB MiniLab in 1990, the tempo of their dancing had changed little.

I have no personal experience with American square dancing in Japan but it has been popular there throughout the last half of the twentieth century. It was introduced by American military personnel in the late 1950's but grew in popularity with the Japanese in much the same manner that it did in Germany. My caller friends who have been there assure me that the Japanese have an uncommon skill with the technical aspects of square dancing and that they dance with considerable style and grace as well. One difference between clubs in the United States and those in Japan is the scarcity of couples' clubs. Most Japanese dancers join the club as individuals and there is considerable changing of partners for each tip. The lack of balance in the number of men and women has often led Japanese dancers to learn the dances in both the left and right couple positions. This "all-position" experience may be a substantial reason for the technical proficiency of the Japanese dancers. One of the early international members of CALLERLAB was Tac Ozaki from Japan who first attended a CALLERLAB convention in 1979.

## WEEKENDS AND FESTIVALS

The distinction between conventions and festivals is not sharply drawn. In general a dance event that uses volunteer services of some or all of the local callers in its region is called a convention. Events that hire a paid staff of callers and round dance leaders are commonly referred to as festivals. Both of these are likely to involve more than one day of dancing and usually include more than one hall with different programs offered in each. The National Square Dance Convention has always used unpaid, volunteer callers and considers its region to be, at a minimum, the whole United States. It has, throughout its fifty years of existence, nearly always included a substantial representation from other regions of the world. There are many state conventions and regional festivals. One of the earliest of the modern square dance festivals grew out of the Atlantic Convention first held in Boston, Massachusetts in 1955. After a second year in Boston, the organizers decided to move it to other cities. It went to Atlantic City, New Jersey, Washington, D.C., Toronto, Ontario, Canada and Baltimore,

Maryland. In each city after Boston, when the Atlantic Convention moved on, it was replaced by a festival which continued to operate for many years. Several are still held annually even as this is written.

Weekend and summer week-long square dance institutes also have a long history. Lloyd Shaw's summer meetings were the models for many. The traditional dancers also had summer dance camps. It was at one of these run by Ralph Page in Peterborough, New Hampshire that I first tried calling in 1949. Al Brundage ran both summer weeks and weekend events in the early 1950's to bring the early modern callers to the Northeast. Bob Osgood had begun his summer weeks at Asilomar in Northern California almost as soon as he started the magazine. These institutes and weekends were popular with the most eager dancers. The people who went to such intense dance events were the most dedicated. They enjoyed participating in the company of others who were equally enthusiastic. For the callers who ran these events, they were considerably more profitable than one-night club dances.

Callers found a ready market for weekends with the exploding square dance population. They usually provided a single program of dancing with a staff of two or more callers and a round dance leader. Dancing was scheduled morning, afternoon and evening and usually included a workshop to improve the dancer's skills and sessions to teach a couple of new round dances. The quality of the dancing was expected to be better at weekends than at conventions and, after the CALLERLAB dance programs were established, the focus on a particular program of dancing appealed strongly to the most committed dancers. The number of such events was expanding as we entered the 1980's. A listing of vacation facilities in 1980 that offered dance events each year included forty locations in twenty-one states and Canada. A listing of "Big Events of 1985" in *Sets in Order* included more than 200 events and only a small share of them was what we have identified as conventions.

## RETIREMENT PARKS

Another business that found an effective connection to the square dance activity was the mobile home parks in popular retirement/vacation areas. Jerry Haag had, in 1973, been one of the first to take a full-time position as resident square dance caller in one of these parks. Once other parks learned of the compatibility between their customers and square dancing, they hired full-time callers. Parks with large and beautiful dance halls proliferated throughout Florida, South Texas and Arizona. It was a perfect fit. The generation of people from which square dancing had been recruiting for three decades was reaching retirement age. The retirees found an activity that could keep them interested and active. Many visited other nearby parks and danced several times each week during the winter season. Callers found a steady, profitable employment during a period when travel up north was difficult. During this period crowds at the park dances were huge. It was not unusual to find twenty to forty squares at a Monday morning workshop or class. And sixty-square evening dances were common. Much of this dancing was on weekdays and many of the callers were able to travel on weekends to work at festivals in addition to their regular weekday work in the parks. These programs attracted many of the best known traveling callers. It was a good time for both dancers and callers.

## VACATION TRAVEL

The square dance travel business was thriving as we entered the 1980's. It was started many years earlier with vacation trips for square dancers run by Bob Osgood and Al Brundage. As the activity reached a peak of popularity, the availability of this kind of travel grew vigorously. Dancers found that other dancers shared many of their own interests and made good travel companions. The personal qualities and commitment required to complete a square dance class and become a square dancer meant that those who did were very likely to be tolerant and socially comfortable. They were not complainers and they accepted responsibility for themselves. They were fun to travel with. The dancer population was also aging and retiring from their lifetime employment. They had the time to travel and they did it enthusiastically. The volume of ads for such trips in the magazines increased noticeably during the early 1980's. In the April 1985 issue of *Sets in Order*, an extensive list of available trips for square dancers was included in an article about this trend. It showed a total of sixty-nine tours and cruises divided between Europe, Japan, the Orient, the South Pacific and North America as destinations. This business continued strongly through the 1990's. Even as we enter the new millennium there are many cruises and overseas tours being offered.

## COMPUTERS

Yet another change that began to spread in the 1980's was the use of computers. In 1975, Clark Baker, then a senior at Massachusetts Institute of Technology, chose the programming of a computer to write square dance routines as a senior project. Clark had very recently learned to dance and with help from his caller, Don Beck, he undertook the project which he described in the abstract this way:

The information necessary to produce on paper danceable, computer-generated Modern Western style square dance hash sequences is investigated...

The importance of his conclusions was not widely appreciated until many years later. His thesis expressed them this way:

Within limits, the computer can generate and resolve danceable hash sequences. The major problem with the sequences is that they are too difficult to do. This stems from two reasons. First, the sequences contain certain calls in orders not usually heard. Secondly, the caller [a reference to the computer program] is not very good at naming people and names them in ways not usually heard. While the second is definitely a problem and should be improved, the first may or may not be a problem depending on the use of the generated sequences. They should be used with dancers who are sure of the level and want interesting, unusual choreography and not with dancers who are unsure of themselves.

During the development of his computer program Clark brought some of the sequences it had written to a meeting of our Tri-State Callers Association. We formed a square and tried to walk through - not dance, just to walk through - the sequences. We found we could not. The computer's selection of calls, while perfectly legitimate and in accordance with the definitions, were not combinations that were commonly used. It was this experience that first brought to my attention the importance of what the dancers find familiar. Sequences of calls tend to be repeated regularly by callers far more than the callers or the dancers realize. Those sequences are learned by experienced dancers and can be executed successfully. Sequences or combinations of calls that are not common are very likely to cause breakdown on the floor. Some callers realized this fact intuitively but most did not. The experience with Clark's routines was to begin a learning process that took a couple of decades to bring about understanding of this effect even among the caller coaches. That experience also led indirectly to the eventual publication of the CALLERLAB *Standard Applications* books in the 1990's.

Clark's program was the first step along the path toward what has become the widespread practice of using computers as tools in the choreographic creation process. His work was done on an Institute mainframe computer. In the early 1980's, he created a program on the mainframe computer where he worked that would keep track of the dancer positions as he created choreographic routines. It was this capability that would prove most valuable for callers. Personal computers were not to become adequate for the task for several more years. When they did become available, others soon found ways to use them. The earliest personal computers were not very user friendly and those who would use them for development of choreography had to be both skilled computer operators and skilled choreographers. The first developers of this application were Don Beck, who did his work on a Macintosh, Bill Ackerman who also came through the Mass. Institute of Technology square dance group, Tech Squares, and Vic Cedar. As the tools developed, they became much more widely available and more widely used, particularly among callers working in the Advanced and Challenge programs.

## DANCER MIXING - THE NUMBER SYSTEMS

Another application for computers in the square dance world was first addressed without the help of the machines. As the dancing became more complex, the variation of skills and level of commitment within the dancer community presented problems. Particularly in learning situations such as workshops in the Advanced groups and in classes even for beginning dancers there were some who learned much more quickly than others. This was apparent from the very earliest days of modern square dancing. It was, in fact, uncanny in even the earliest classes to see how quickly the best dancers identified each other and how certainly they ended up in the same squares together. We had always used simple ways of mixing the dancers including the scatter promenade and "Head couples Pass Thru and go find a new square." This method wasn't adequate for the Challenge groups. In the mid 1970's Bill Mills, a dancer from New Jersey who was a mathematician, and the Square Dance Systems people in New England both devised charts to accomplish this mixing. Their systems required the dancers to consult the charts between each tip to discover which square they should dance in for the next tip. It was cumbersome but did assure that no couple had to dance with the weakest of the others more than a fair share of the evening. When computers became generally available they were applied to the task. Don Beck created a set of cards that could be handed out to dancers as they arrived. Many other variations of this method have been created and marketed. With the greater availability of these systems and of computers that can be brought to the dance, their use for assigning dancers to different squares has become quite common.

## DIVERSITY

Diversity in American society was spreading rapidly as we entered the 1980's. Mixing of people with different ethnic backgrounds was both a legal requirement and a social goal. Square dancing had been isolated from this trend. In most areas it wasn't a conscious exclusion. In fact, in a limited way, square dancing had been a very democratic recreation. Dancers tended to be concerned only with the dancing skills of other dancers. The western style costumes that were nearly universal tended to obscure many of the cues that people normally used to identify social status. Bankers, lawyers, laborers, tradesmen, rich and not very rich all mingled in square dance clubs. They often had no idea what the other club members did for work or what their educational background was.

With few exceptions, however, the clubs had very little ethnic diversity. In some industrial areas like Detroit there were a few clubs with primarily black membership and there were occasional black members in clubs with predominantly white membership. There were a few black callers. There were some areas in which black dancers were not welcome in predominantly white square dance clubs. The laws against discrimination in public facilities that came into existence early in the life of modern square dancing led, in those areas, to widespread use of non-public facilities and very limited public advertising of square dance classes. Sexual discrimination was obviously not a big issue among dancers and there were a few women callers, too. This is, however, a couple activity. People who did not have partners did not find themselves widely accepted. Clubs were formed specifically for single dancers. The B&B's (Bachelors and Bachelorettes) which originated in California was formed as an association of singles clubs. A National Singles Square Dance Convention was started in the early 1970's.

The National Association of Gay and Lesbian Square Dance Clubs was formed in 1984. Square dancing specifically designated for gays began in the late 1970's. By the mid-1980's there were gay square dance clubs in many of the major cities of the United States. The first National Gay Square Dance Convention was held in Seattle in 1984. Square dancing has become very popular with this segment of society. It serves the same valuable social functions that it has for non-gay club members for several decades. Particularly among younger gay people, modern square dancing has provided a comfortable and non-threatening social meeting ground. In these groups it is common that men and women learn to dance in both the left and right couple positions. This flexibility has resulted in an automatic "all-position" dancing skill. As we enter the new millennium, this is one of very few segments of the square dance community that is showing strong growth. Even in this group, however, convention attendance which grew steadily until the early 1990's has remained nearly constant since.

# CHAPTER 14 - ALL POSITION DANCING,
## AN ELUSIVE GOAL

CALLERLAB leaders, many of whom were traveling callers, were concerned that restricting the use of new calls would lead to considerable dancer boredom. Most of the traveling callers had been using the endless supply of new calls as a major component of the variety they felt was necessary. Now they had agreed to call dances without relying on new calls. How much variety was necessary and appropriate would become a continuing but often hidden issue. Even before the formation of CALLERLAB, there were some who resisted the trend toward introducing new calls at every dance. They preferred, instead, to provide variety in their dance programs by using the "standard" calls in a wider variety of setups.

One of the most outspoken advocates of this approach was Frank Lane. Throughout the 1960's when others were introducing new calls at a furious pace, Frank continued to program his dances in the way that was common at the start of that decade. He began with a fairly simple basic pattern and then introduced variety by changing the boy/girl arrangement or the setup of the formation in which the standard calls were used. It was a philosophy that grew out of the leadership of Ed Gilmore. When Les Gotcher introduced the use of new calls as a basis for programming his dances, Ed Gilmore resisted this technique and urged us to rely on more effective use of a standard vocabulary.

Frank Lane's enthusiasm for use of calls in widely varied setups made him an obvious choice to be chairman of the All Position Dancing Committee which was established by CALLERLAB in 1978. He and some others were convinced that using new calls rather than position or setup variety in dance programming had reduced the ability of the dancers to accomplish calls used in non-standard setups. This was one of the concerns underlying the "How We Dance" topic which was one of three major subjects addressed at the first Convention in 1974. Jack Lasry had expressed some reservations about the extent of variety that should be provided, particularly for the people he had identified as "mainstream" dancers. He was made Co-chairman of the committee.

Many callers believed that an essential component of modern square dancing was the ability of dancers to respond to the calls as they were presented. The whole premise behind the establishment of a standard list of calls was that callers could and should use those calls in a variety of different ways and that dancers should be able to execute the calls successfully even from unusual places in a formation or with an unusual arrangement of boys and girls. In the fifteen years since the first introduction of choreographic control methods there had been a transition from routines memorized by both the caller and the dancers to choreography that the caller changed as he or she called it. While this was true among most of the active traveling callers, it had not yet taken hold with local club callers. Most of them were still using memorized routines.

The callers who joined CALLERLAB were the most active even among local club callers. The matter of position variety was near and dear to their hearts. They enjoyed exploring the many ways in which the calls could be used. There were among us a few, a very few, who began to be concerned about how much more difficult it was to learn to do the calls from all these different setups. At the 1976 Convention I shared in the discussions that led to the resolution establishing the Mainstream Plus program. (The name was later changed to Plus, without the "Mainstream" to reduce confusion.) Lee Kopman, who was the chairman of the Dance Level Identification Committee, and I had agreed in private discussion that any adequate dance identification system would need to include not only the vocabulary of calls but also the variety of positions in which those calls were to be used. It was that understanding that led to use of the term "All Position Dancing" in the resolution that established the Mainstream Plus Program. We also agreed that an understanding of that aspect of dance difficulty was not common among callers. We knew that most callers were still using memorized routines that they took out of publications. Their awareness of the increased difficulty that resulted from an unusual setup for a call was limited at best. For most callers it was an issue to which they had given little or no thought. The curriculum that had been accepted for caller training did not mention difficulty as one of the elements of dancing to consider when programming a dance. Nevertheless, it was clear to several of us on the committee that one component of any program of dancing aimed at more committed dancers would have to recognize the importance of the setup in which calls were used as well as the vocabulary of calls.

The question of position variety was not limited to the Plus program. Frank Lane's committee was encouraging callers to teach and use all the calls, even those on the Mainstream list, from a wide variety of setups. They believed that callers should be teaching most calls from several setups in class. The CALLERLAB program lists included a recommendation to "not teach from just a single position/formation." The June 1979 Program List included two columns on the reverse side of the sheet. The first column was a list of the Plus I and Plus II calls. The second column included the following comments and list:

### ALL POSITION DANCING:

APD figures for use during MS teaching and dancing may include some judicious use of the following calls. (Please note that we refer to a Mainstream Dancer as one who dances once a week or perhaps twice a month). No attempt has been made to include the Q.S. or either + list in the following APD variations.

Do Sa Do - Same Sex
Pass Thru - all variations
Star Family - 2-8 all variations
Star Promenade - all variations of sex
Couples lead right - all variations
Bend the Line - all variations
Grand Square - Use Fractional
Square Thru - as on list but use variety
Cross Trail Thru - normal or ½ sashayed
Slip the Clutch - Normal or from Dixie Style

Ocean Wave Family - all variations
Swing Thru Family - all variations
Trade Family - all variations
Flutterwheel - all variations
Sweep a Quarter - right & left variations
Veer Left & Right - all variations
Run Family - all variations
Circulate Family - all variations but not facing lines at MS
Pass to the Center - all variations
Spin the Top - all variations but not left handed at MS

Trade By - all variations
Zoom/Substitute - all variations including back-to-back or crawdad
Wheel & Deal - all variations
Centers In - all variations
Cast Off 3/4 - vary the casters
Cloverleaf - all variations
Slide Thru - normal & half sashayed only
Peel Off - all variations

Tag Family - all variations
Walk & Dodge - all variations
Scootback - all variations
Fan the Top - all variations
Hinge - all variations
Recycle - from waves but please no hands

Keep them flowing and try to build on what the dancers know. Do not try to clobber them. Please teach according to the approved definition of CALLERLAB. Apply the same approach to the use of APD during the QS and + lists. If the variation is not listed here, then please do not use it for the MS level dance.

The "QS" in that listing was a reference to the Quarterly Selection plan established in 1974 for selecting experimental calls to be used by callers wishing to try calls that were not included on any of the lists.

This list and the closing admonition represent quite clearly the thinking of the leading callers as we headed into the 1980's at the peak of the popularity of modern square dancing. It is quite likely, however, that the majority of callers working in their own towns and cities across America and Canada were not calling this kind of choreography. The techniques of choreographic management that made choreographic flexibility possible were not widely practiced. Many callers could substitute memorized modules into a standard routine but the limitation was still how much they could memorize. What was later to be known as extemporaneous calling was far from common among club callers in 1979. Most dancers were being taught the routines that their caller had memorized. Their exposure to position variety was quite limited. Perhaps it was the frustration of the traveling callers as they tried to live with the limitation on new calls resulting from the acceptance of the CALLERLAB Mainstream list that led to encouragement toward All Position Dancing.

Whatever the motive for promoting APD, it was soon clear that the dancers didn't like it. In the CALLERLAB Board of Governors meeting minutes in March of 1980, Jack Lasry was quoted as follows:

Discussion: Jack Lasry reported that, through reader comments in *Sets in Order* magazine, he has become aware of the dissatisfaction of the dancer with the APD concept. As a consequence, he has concluded that the APD concept should be minimized at the level of the average dancer, and expanded at the higher dancing levels.

Frank Lane suggested that the committee needs to come together and determine the meaning of APD. He stated that his concept was that it is a philosophy of learning and not a matter of creative choreography.

The APD philosophy was to become a continuing issue in modern square dancing.

At the 1980 CALLERLAB Convention, a year after publication of the 1979 program list showing that most Mainstream calls could be used "from all variations," the All Position Dancing Committee reviewed the results of a questionnaire it had prepared and sent out to the committee members. Apparently not everyone had the same idea of how dancers would deal with all position use of the Mainstream calls. Limited positions were identified for the use of eighteen of the then sixty-nine Mainstream calls. Jack Lasry went on in his report of the committee's work saying:

I feel, however, that the most important part of the committee response is reflected in the philosophy of all position dancing as it relates to the MAINSTREAM DANCER. There are many opinions regarding the depth of choreography at the mainstream level and even callers will not agree 100%. Let me list some of the comments received.

1. Why APD at all at the mainstream? Mainstream does not need the complication inflicted upon a fun time that is the basis of the mainstream program.

2. Older or long time dancers who have not been exposed to APD from class thru club dancing greatly reject the use of all position dancing. "I'm a boy and I want to dance a boy's part!!!"

3. Dancers taught from class level accept APD as part of learning to Square Dance and voice no objection. One important problem is that the length of class time may have to be increased in order to properly include basics from all positions.

1. All position dancing at Mainstream should be very simple and
   limited to only a few easy basics. Don't complicate mainstream
   any further, it is enough to teach 69 basics in the 30 - 40 weeks
   of class. Call it Limited Position Dancing.

5. CALLERLAB has received much of the blame for the increased
   use of APD (Comments from dancers in [the magazines.])

6. Develop a complete handbook for teaching mainstream
   including how to teach and use APD during the class program.

So, you see we really have more to consider than a list of basics to
include in the mainstream program from all positions.

My conclusion is that we should establish a very minimum APD
program to be taught with the beginners classes and at Mainstream
dances.

The callers' enthusiasm for use of a wide variety of setups for the standard
call vocabulary was not warmly received by the dancers. But there was a
powerful belief among callers that their customers would (or, probably more
correctly, should) enjoy this All Position Dancing as much as they, the
callers, did. The APD Committee, then chaired by Gregg Anderson,
responded to the dancer complaints by recommending, after the 1982
Convention, that the APD Committee be dissolved. The Board of
Governors chose, instead, to combine the APD Committee and the Teaching
Committee into a Dance By Definition (DBD) Committee with Co-
Chairmen Ernie Kinney, Frank Lane and Gregg Anderson. In fact, only the
name changed. Dance By Definition was widely understood by both callers
and dancers to mean exactly the same thing as All Position Dancing. The
only slight change was a stronger attempt to encourage callers to teach more
than a single set-up when a new call was introduced in class. The goal of
both APD and DBD was to encourage the widest possible application of the
definitions of each call as a regular part of the dancing experience. The
response from dancers was strongly negative. Many felt that the concept
meant mostly that men were dancing the ladies' part of calls.

I was one of a small segment of callers who were concerned early that our
fascination with complexity was a problem. At the 1980 CALLERLAB
Convention in Miami, Florida one of the sessions was a debate led by Bill
Peters and me with the title "Programming for Survival." The description of

this session that Bill and I wrote for the convention program included the following:

> Jim is certain that callers' fascination with geometric puzzles is one of the major reasons that we have been willing to tolerate drop-out rates of 80% of class graduates in the first year. Callers force dancers to seek choreographic challenge by offering no alternative and by believing that those who move on to further levels of complexity are better dancers.

And:

> Bill Peters holds a somewhat different view and will contribute to the discussion his belief that choreographic challenge is an important part of any square dance program and that APD [All Position Dancing] variation is only one of many ways in which a caller can provide such challenge. He would like to see choreographic challenge presented in ways that are appropriate for the skill of the dancers present at any dance - but he <u>does</u> believe that most dancers enjoy, and therefore prefer, their caller to provide at least some challenge.

While encouragement for All Position Dancing didn't find favor with everyone, it had a wide enough influence to change modern square dancing significantly. Just the fact that callers now had to program their dances without new calls led to increased exploration of the ways the standard calls could be used. A few of us were concerned that the new approach was making a major change in the difficulty of this recreation. Kip Garvey described the effect of the growing difficulty of modern square dancing in an article he prepared to hand out at the 1985 CALLERLAB Convention. In a paragraph headed "Difficulty factor too high" he wrote:

> With the implementation of the <u>APD Concept</u> into the dancing, along with its descendant, the DBD [Dance by Definition] Concept, our classes took on a new dimension. We now have one of the purest forms of an IQ Test ever developed. We introduce an abstract concept, give it a new name, and expect dancers to apply that concept to continually changing circumstances (formation and arrangements). If we were an independent testing agency, which we are not, we would have succeeded in putting together a very meaningful IQ Test. Results? Only those with the highest

propensity to understand and achieve, successfully complete the square dance program.

Several of us believed that we had made square dancing so complicated that we had restricted our supply of potential customers only to those people who could be interested in solving fairly complex puzzles. We continually urged the development of easier ways for people to become square dancers. That view, however, was less then popular with many callers whose own enjoyment of square dancing was mostly the excitement of creating choreographic puzzles.

## QUARTERLY EMPHASIS CALLS

Another way that CALLERLAB encouraged callers to adopt the All Position philosophy was the Quarterly Emphasis call program. Starting in March of 1976, immediately after acceptance of the Mainstream program, the Quarterly Movements Committee started selecting a call or two from the Mainstream program for particular attention by callers during each quarter of the year. These were in addition to the experimental calls. They continued the recommendation to review a call from the program until 1978 when the name was changed to Quarterly Selection Committee and responsibility for selecting emphasis calls was taken over by the Mainstream Committee. The emphasis calls were identified in the newsletter *Direction* along with choreographic routines showing how to use the calls in "more than one way" as the program list suggested. To appreciate the variety that was being recommended, consider the following listing of the starting setups in the choreography presented for the emphasis call Fan The Top in September1978. (Note that the terms "Formation" and "Arrangement" did not become part of the accepted language of caller training until more than five years later. I have used them here to show a degree of complexity that was not widely understood in 1978.)

| **Formation** | **Arrangement** |
|---|---|
| Parallel Waves | Normal (Girls in Center) |
| Parallel Waves | Boy and Girl in Center |
| Tidal Wave | Half Sashayed (Boys Center) |
| Tidal Wave | Girls in Center |
| Facing Couples | Normal Couples |
| Tidal Two-Faced Lines | Boy and Girl in Center |
| Double Pass Thru | Normal Couples |
| Parallel Two-Faced Lines | Normal Couples |
| Parallel Two-Faced Lines | Boy and Girl in Center |

The Direction article presenting the selection followed the choreography examples with this paragraph:

> We urge all of you to work with these two calls [The other selection was Peel Off] during the last quarter of this year. They are good calls that form the basis of some other calls that we call for the dancers but we have ignored their widespread use. Perhaps if we get creative in our own programs, we will see a greater use of these calls at festivals and dances.

It has often been said that CALLERLAB is an organization that serves the interests of the full-time traveling callers more than those of local club callers. Statements like that paragraph provide some justification for that idea.

# CHAPTER 15 - DANCING CHANGES

The emphasis on APD along with a growing interest by callers in Advanced dancing resulted in a substantial upheaval in the modern square dance world. The new-call approach to variety had been widely used and was easy for both callers and dancers. Callers could plug a new call into routines they had memorized. Dancers were, for the most part, taught the new calls - and the routine in which they would be used - before they were expected to dance them. There wasn't much variation in the way the standard calls that made up the routine were used. Pressure to limit use of new calls combined with strong interest in variety from both dancer and caller leaders put the local club caller and many of his or her customers in a bind. Teachers of callers, almost all of whom were CALLERLAB founding members, were mostly in agreement that dancers should be taught the widest possible application of call definitions. Many club callers who had been happy, and whose clubs had been successful, with essentially the same dance called every Saturday night with a few new calls added, were encouraged to use the standard calls in ways their dancers had never seen. The dancers who were happy with "the same old stuff" were not the ones who spoke to callers. Many of them just gave up square dancing.

The most significant difference between modern square dancing and its traditional counterpart is the variety of the choreography. There are two major components of that variety, the number of calls that are used and the way in which they are used. As we quoted in Chapter 7, Jay King described the nature of the modern approach to square dancing this way:

In this kind of choreography, dancers learn only a number of 'basic' movements (instead of learning entire dance patterns as they once did) and the caller, by use of these basics, moves the dancers through a series of 'grid,' line and column patterns <u>toward an ending known only to himself</u>. While dancers have stopped memorizing dance patterns, however, callers still use large numbers of memorized routines which today's dancers can often figure out after one time through and can anticipate the movements if the routine is called a second time.

Modern square dance callers have always believed in choreographic variety and we expect to provide that variety by changing the dance pattern as we call it. Ever since Jay wrote those words in the 1960's, callers have been encouraged "to avoid calling the same routine a second time." There has been an almost universal subliminal, and often conscious, worry that modern square dancers would be bored if a dance routine was repeated even once. In fact, many experienced callers have learned that most dancers' memory of a routine is erased by doing some other routine. The risk of boredom is thereby easily overcome. Nevertheless, there has been strong encouragement to avoid repeating any routine within the same tip.

In traditional square dancing there is a smaller vocabulary, but a substantial variety in the way the calls are used is possible because the dancers are taught the dance pattern before they are expected to dance it. The routine they have learned is then repeated at least once and often four times. Disappearance of the "walk through" from modern square dancing sometime in the 1970's meant the end of any hint to the dancers of the pattern they were about to dance, at least in the patter half of the tip. It was still common until the last decade or so for the singing call choreography to be essentially the same for all four choruses.

As we have mentioned earlier, there has always been a range of ability among the dancers. Two major factors contribute to dancer success in executing a dance routine. These are frequency of dancing and the ability to apply the definition of a call in a wide range of situations. The two are, of course, related. The more a person dances the more likely they are to have encountered calls in unusual setups. For every call there is a standard way in which it is commonly used. For nearly every call the standard use is one that starts from a normal couple orientation with the man on the left and the woman on the right. There are also common formations of the square in which the calls are used. These are called, in the language of caller technology, arrangement and formation. They are two of the four terms that fully identify the choreographic situation in a square at any point in a routine. The other two are sequence and relationship. These four terms were defined and accepted at a meeting of Accredited Caller Coaches held in Dallas, Texas in 1981. The agreements reached at this meeting would allow publication in 1986 of the *Curriculum Guideline for Caller Training* by the CALLERLAB Caller Training Committee. Formation and arrangement together are referred to as the setup in which a call is used. Variations in these two factors determine to a large extent the difficulty of a choreographic routine. They are the components of the dance experience that are referred to by the term All Position Dancing. In the earliest decade of modern square dancing such variations were rare. Sometimes the youngest or most eager dancers, myself included, danced in a square with the man/woman positions reversed. This could be either one or all four couples dancing half-sashayed and it was called "Arky" dancing. It was a way of making the dancing more interesting.

Comparison of dance routines presented in the most widespread source of written choreography, the *Sets in Order* Workshop section, illustrates somewhat the kind of choreographic change that was taking place. In the March 1976 issue, as was the magazine's usual practice, the choreography used by a particular caller was featured. Eleven routines were written out each starting from a squared set and ending with a Left Allemande. These two routines are typical of the eleven:

| | |
|---|---|
| Sides right & left thru | Heads lead right |
| Sides roll a half sashay | Veer to the left |
| Heads square thru four hands around | Couples circulate |
| | Bend the line |
| Step to an ocean wave | Right and left thru |
| Swing thru | Pass thru |
| Cast off three quarters | Wheel and deal |
| Ends circulate | Center four pass thru |
| Centers trade | Swing thru |
| Boys run right | Cast off three quarters |
| Bend the line | Split circulate |
| Star thru | Boys run |
| Dive thru | Right and left thru |
| Pass thru | Curlique |
| Star thru | Coordinate |
| Right and left thru | Half Tag |
| Pass thru | Trade and roll |
| Wheel and deal | Right and left thru |

Zoom
New centers pass thru
Swing thru
Turn thru
Left Allemande

Dive thru
Pass thru
Star thru
Pass thru
Tag the line
Leaders U turn back
Star thru
Slide thru
Left Allemande

In fact these two routines use all but a half dozen of the calls that were used in the whole eleven routines. The routines are made up mostly of calls on the *Sets in Order* Basic list with occasional appearances of less common calls. They also use setups for those calls that are, for the most part, the normal use of the call. The boys are on the left and the girls on the right in nearly every case. The one exception in these examples is the boy-facing-boy Swing Thru that followed the first Square Thru. The fact that the sequences were written out fully is not unusual for the time. There are two ways that might have come about. Either the caller had them written out in his personal collection of material and sent them to the magazine or he could have copied them from a tape of a dance (or dances) that he had called. It is far more likely that he had them written out in his own collection. It is also likely that he would have read them as he called. There is nothing in either of these routines or in the other nine that would not have been regarded as completely normal and usual at the time. Even the half-sashayed Square Thru was common in 1976 although it has become much less so since. These routines are a reflection of what was being called at many club dances in 1976.

Nearly a decade later, in the *Sets in Order* issue of March 1985, the Workshop section was still presenting square dance routines for callers. They did not, however, just reproduce typical routines. This issue featured "Half Tag Variations" presented by Bill Peters. His introductory paragraph starts:

It is a curious fact that while most callers call a full tag the line right (or left) fairly regularly, they hardly ever seem to call a half tag right (or left). This is curious because the action of a half tag right is just as danceable as a full tag right, and it is certainly also true that the add-on command to face right or left or in or out, after completing a half tag, is every bit as "legal" as it is at the end of a full tag the line. It is, therefore, reasonably safe to assume that most dancers probably do not encounter a half tag right very often these days - which means that call may serve as a logical candidate for an interesting Mainstream theme tip.

The format of presenting routines in the magazine had changed but here are two of the eleven that were presented there:

One and three square thru...swing thru...Boys run...half tag right...swing thru...Recycle...veer left...couples circulate Half tag right...Swing thru...recycle Square thru three quarters...trade by...Allemande left

One and three right and left thru...Flutterwheel...pass the ocean Girls trade...girls run...half tag right...Pass thru...swing thru...boys run... Bend the line...pass the ocean...Girls trade...Girls run...half tag right...Touch one quarter...scoot back...Boys fold...All double pass thru...girls trade...All star thru...couples circulate...Half tag right...Right and left grand

In 1976 there is little concern with the extent of variety in the material shown. There was no introductory comment and no purpose other than to provide routines that might be danced successfully by club dancers of the day. By 1985 the material presented was described in the introductory comment as a way callers could provide more "interesting" dancing experiences for their customers. Each of the routines incorporated various setups for the featured call but the primary variety was the use of a call that is not used regularly - the Half Tag Face Left or Right. At the same time Bill felt he had to point out that while his routines were unusual they were, nevertheless, "legal." By 1985 there was beginning to be some questioning of just how "unusual" a call use could or should be. The common use of Half Tag at that time was to follow it with either Trade and Roll or with Scoot Back. The addition of a facing direction was not usual. Another element of interest in the 1985 choreography was that half of the routines ended directly into a Grand Right and Left without the Allemande Left. In 1976 all routines ended with Allemande Left.[16]

---

[16] By the end of the century this trend had gone a step further. Many routines ended with all the dancers in their original place without using either the Allemande or the Grand Right and Left.

Encouragement to make the choreography more interesting by a well known traveling caller was understood by many callers as a recommendation that they should be providing this kind of interesting material for their customers. Bill was also an active teacher of callers and, in his schools and most others, students were always encouraged to strive for greater variety in their programs. Variety was understood by nearly everyone to mean using calls in ways that were not "usual" for the dancers.

That this approach was not accepted by all callers is illustrated by a conversation that took place at a party in our room one night at the 1987 Convention in New Orleans. One of the most successful and popular traveling callers of all time is Marshall Flippo. "Flip" has had little interest in the technology of calling. He is a wonderful entertainer with an instinctive ability to suit his choreography to the ability of the dancers. My friend, Johnny Wedge was a student of Marshall's in the early 1960's in one of the few caller training programs Marshall ever took part in. At the party both Johnny and Marshall were sitting on the sofa listening to an extended technical discussion between Bill Peters, Al Stevens and me about the importance of FASR which is an acronym for Formation, Arrangement, Sequence and Relationship. Marshall nudged Johnny and said "Hey, do you have any idea what they're talking about." Johnny said he thought he knew what the terms were but wasn't sure of what they meant. Marshall's reply was "Heck. I don't even know the words. I just pick up the mike and start calling."

## DANCER SEGREGATION SPREADS

As we entered the 1980's, the division of the dancer population was being extended. Modern square dancing had branched off from its traditional forbears in the 1950's. By the end of the 1960's, the *Sets in Order* Basic and Extended Basic program identification had recognized further segregation within the modern branch of the activity. The distinction between dancers was firmly established by CALLERLAB's creation of the Mainstream and Plus programs. Even before that there were dancers using a vocabulary of calls much larger than the approximately one hundred that would make up the CALLERLAB lists. These were often tape groups of a square or two that met in someone's home to learn the extra calls from tape recordings. In 1977 CALLERLAB had recognized the existence of dance programs called Advanced, Basic Challenge and Extended Challenge. All of them were based on call vocabularies much larger than the Mainstream and Plus lists. The new organization did not accept any responsibility for managing those additional programs until the mid-1980's and even as we entered the twenty-first century the Challenge programs (C-1 through C-4) were not under the full control of CALLERLAB.   Slowly, during the 1980's, the structure of the Advanced and Challenge programs was made more formal.   Many clubs were formed to dance only the Advanced or Challenge programs and, usually, they did not sponsor classes for new dancers.

This division of the dancer population created some conflict within the dancer community.   In areas where Advanced dancing was available it tended to bleed off the better dancers - or at least those most eager for more challenge - from the clubs where only the Mainstream or Plus programs were danced.   Over the years there has been strong criticism of CALLERLAB for establishing separately identified dance programs.   There is clearly the feeling among many that the identification of the programs caused the segmentation of the dance community.   There is ample evidence, however, to establish that the division was already underway before the CALLERLAB programs were established.   One of the concerns of the founders even before the first convention was that there would be several program identification systems established in different sections of the United States.   Had that happened, the task of winning acceptance of a worldwide, or even nationwide, program identification would have become much more difficult if not impossible.

It was not only the Advanced dancing that was dividing the dancers.   There was also a considerable enthusiasm in many areas for the Plus program or at least for some of the Plus program calls.   It was clear that in most of California, many of the northeastern states and in many areas in the southeastern United States, particularly in Florida, the number of clubs that were dancing the Mainstream program was shrinking while the number of clubs dancing the Plus program was growing.   No one has ever fully explained why this phenomenon occurred.   The "rush to Plus" as it was called was much less common in the central United States and did not occur until much later, if at all, in the Pacific Northwest and most areas outside the United States.   By the start of the 1990's the areas that I have named in this paragraph had effectively eliminated Mainstream as an available dance program.   Anyone learning modern square dancing in those areas had to learn at least several of the Plus calls in addition to the calls on the Mainstream list.   Otherwise, they would be unable to dance at most of the club dances in the area.

Many hours of discussion have been held among callers trying to understand the "rush to Plus" phenomenon.   Someone once said "It is an economic law of nature that any growing market will segment." Certainly the separation of dancers by the intensity of their involvement had begun long before any dance programs were identified. There are many who explain it as a natural tendency to move through any graduated set. We learn as children that we move from one grade to the next and we are urged always to improve our proficiency in any field. When the progression of square dance programs was established, it produced an urge among dancers to move through that progression. Perhaps the desire to know more calls was left over from the 1960's when the more active dancers learned more of the new calls that were taught at nearly every dance. That era certainly reinforced the idea that better dancers knew more calls. By the time the CALLERLAB dance programs were established, the Advanced and Challenge identification had already been applied to dancers whose vocabulary of calls in regular use was much larger than the about one hundred that made up the Plus program. Challenge dancers used as many as four hundred calls. This, too, led to the conclusion that better dancers know more calls. The quality of dancing style became less important than the size of the vocabulary.

My own experience demonstrated the strong attraction that a program based on more calls had for the dancers. The invitation-only club that I had started in the late 1960's was dedicated to the use of the (then) standard vocabulary of calls in a wider-than-usual variety of setups. There were several closed clubs in the area and mine was the only one that was not dedicated to teaching new experimental calls. The club attracted some of the most experienced dancers in our area and the membership was always filled to capacity. Within two years after the Plus program was established by CALLERLAB, the club had ceased to exist. I cannot say why the dancers made this choice. While the competing groups were teaching calls identified as experimental, my group competed successfully. As soon as the additional calls became a recognized program, this group of exceptional dancers wanted to participate in that program. Whatever the reason, there is no question that the establishment of a program of dancing "beyond" the Mainstream resulted in a substantial share of the dancers wanting to dance that program.

Another possible way of looking at the rush to Plus phenomenon, at least in the early days of program identification, recognizes that many dancers already knew many of the calls on the Plus program. They were, after all, the most popular of the experimental calls that had been introduced during the previous decade. The most active dancers had been dancing these calls for some time. Those active dancers were also the leaders of square dance clubs. It is no surprise, then, that they wanted their club to be the one that used the larger vocabulary. Those leaders also wanted to be sure that the callers who called for their clubs made full use of the calls on the Plus program. Many of us remember being told emphatically by the club officers who hired us that we were to "call a Plus dance" even if many of the dancers present didn't know the Plus calls.

The worldwide acceptance of the dance programs was one of the most successful accomplishments of CALLERLAB. Square dancing, in particular modern square dancing, had been around almost as long in overseas areas as it had in North America. In the 1980's, though, it began the kind of explosive growth in Australia, Japan and Europe that had happened during the '70's in North America. In those areas the dance programs were adopted eagerly and new dancers were encouraged to stay in groups dancing only the Mainstream program for at least a couple of years before experimenting with Plus. CALLERLAB recommended that approach and it was accepted and followed much more completely in off-shore clubs than in North America. Even in Canada new dancers were much less likely to be encouraged into the Plus program than was true particularly in California and on the east coast of the United States. The growth of square dance popularity outside North America has been attributed by many to the fact that CALLERLAB recommendations for maintaining the availability of Mainstream dancing were followed more closely there. It may only be a consequence of the dancer segregation that was in full flower in the United States before the dance programs were established.

It is certainly possible that the existence of an accepted structure made the development of modern square dancing outside the United States proceed in a more orderly fashion than it did at home. However many other factors were involved and to some extent each non United States region was unique in both the timing and method of introduction of the activity. There has been a tendency to regard the overseas programs as problem free. The blame for the problems that were building in the United States is often attributed to failure to adhere to the CALLERLAB recommendation to keep new dancers in Mainstream-only groups for at least the first year of their dancing life. Nearly everyone agrees the recommended practice is a good one. It is not clear, however, that it is possible to control the movement of new dancers that completely. Often the experienced dancers who bring new recruits to a class also encourage them to move rapidly through the programs to join them dancing in Plus or Advanced groups. Only time will tell whether the recommended approach will prove ultimately to be effective or whether the overseas programs are just a decade behind the United States along the same path.

## SIGHT CALLING SPREADS

Encouragement of increased variety in square dance choreography was not new. Variety is accepted by everyone as a fundamental component of modern square dancing. From the early 1960's when several methods of choreographic management were introduced, caller training has focused on teaching callers to provide variety. Callers and would-be callers have always come to caller schools seeking to learn how to move the dancers through a routine to successful completion. That success is defined as arriving at the end of a routine with the original corner and with the whole square in the right sequence. Callers want to accomplish this without making the effort to memorize routines. They could, of course, read the routines and many do. But there has also been near total agreement among caller coaches that reading the calls cannot be done well enough to provide a good dancing experience.[17]

By 1980 almost every new caller and most of those who wanted continuing education of any kind wanted to learn sight calling. It seemed the easy way to provide lots of choreographic variety without having to memorize very much. Traveling callers increased their use of choreography that appeared, at least, to be created as they called it and still they managed to get the successful squares back to their original corner. The existence of a standard list of calls led callers to expect that the dancers would know those calls. There was an underlying concern that just dancing routines using only the common setups and only calls the dancers knew would be boring. Many callers treated this as justification for using increasingly complicated - and, in my view at least, sometimes downright crazy - choreography. Callers were believing what the dancers had accepted all along, that any dancer who couldn't dance what they were calling must be poorly trained. There was also continuing pressure from the most vocal experienced dancers for more challenging dance routines. It seemed to callers that sight calling was the easiest way to offer the intricate choreography that both they and their customers wanted. In this discussion it is worth noting that the reason most

---

[17] The widespread use of reading by Challenge program callers has called into question this fundamental belief. Those who read in the Challenge programs are skilled in other methods of choreographic control and no one really believes that good calling is possible with reading alone.

challenge callers read is that they do not feel they can provide the variety their customers demand with sight calling.

What sight calling really meant was widely misunderstood. New callers had always come to caller school looking for the magic "key" that would make calling easy. Many of them believed that sight calling was that key and caller schools did little to discourage that belief. Much of the curriculum at most schools was dedicated to teaching student callers how to apply the rules of sight resolution. The technique was hardly a complete solution to the calling "problem." All it offered was a way to return the dancers to a proper relationship at the conclusion of a dance routine. And it didn't require the caller to keep track of the partner/corner relationship all the way through the routine. Essentially sight calling is nothing more than a method for resolving the square after a routine. It does not in itself create, or even facilitate, interesting dance patterns or sequences. In addition, adequate use of the sight method of resolution requires that the caller know the identity of four adjacent people in a <u>successful</u> square.

The earliest users of the sight method assured us that we would have to remember the identity of four people in at least three squares in order to be certain that one of them would be the successful square that we would need. Deuce Williams who was widely admired as an early sight caller told me that he expected to remember the necessary four people in at least five squares when he was calling for non familiar dancers. He could do it. Most of us could not. Some tried to write down the identification information before each tip. Others got to the dance early and watched the pre-rounds to pick out the best dancers. One of the festival callers with a reputation for really intricate choreography always had his wife in a carefully selected square dance right in front of him. All but a very few of the most skilled and experienced callers watched the squares they had chosen very intently to be sure they noticed if that "key" square broke down. Certainly, most of the callers who were new to the sight technique hardly took their eyes off the square they had chosen. They also did everything they could to make sure that the key square was successful. If this meant waiting while that square figured out what to do, no matter - even if the rest of the floor had to wait while they did it.

There was a rush to learn and use sight calling to ease the caller's memory workload. New callers were all taught sight resolution methods and encouraged not to be dependent on memory. Unfortunately, most callers never did become proficient even at sight resolution and while learning those methods they forgot about memorizing. A very common dance routine became a "get-in" to move the dancers to a line or box formation and then a hit-and-miss attempt to resolve the square. One of the most recommended sight resolution methods involved moving the dancers to two-faced lines, checking for partner relationship, getting one or both key couples with their partner by a series of Circulates and Trades and then following a memorized sequence to the Left Allemande. The thought that there should be some dancing between the get-in and the resolution was pretty much forgotten as callers struggled to find the right corner.

There was a wide-spread belief among caller coaches that most of the students who had been to their schools were "sight callers." They didn't give much thought to what these callers called before the resolution. In fact, I discovered that even this belief was false. In 1986 I took a five-month motor home trip around the United States and western Canada. Most weekends during that trip I was hired to conduct a caller clinic for a caller association. I came in contact with more than three hundred callers in widely scattered locations and most had been to at least one school. I discovered that, in fact, no more than 20 percent of them could resolve a square successfully and reliably. If I interrupted their calling and inserted a call that they didn't expect, the resolution was likely to take a long time if it was accomplished at all. Yet, when I asked how many were sight callers, most raised their hands.

Against this background of limited skill with the sight method there was a shrinking use of memorized dance routines. At the same time the most admired callers, those who traveled and were the featured festival callers, used choreography that was growing in complexity. They believed in the All Position ideas being encouraged by CALLERLAB. Most of them had been calling long enough to have memorized a substantial collection of interesting routines. The sight resolution skills that they learned freed them from total dependence on memory. They could present choreographic segments from their memorized collection and, when memory failed, complete the resolution with sight. Since they didn't call for the same people every week they could also use a new routine night after night until it was perfected. The less skilled and experienced callers tried to copy these routines but without the skill, preparation and opportunity for practice of those they were copying. Dancer success rates dropped. Even skilled club callers face a different problem. They call for the same people every week. Providing a continuing supply of changing choreography week after week was a much more challenging task. The party line, though, was that they had to keep that choreography changing or their dancers would be bored.

The spread of sight calling also had its effect on the dancing experience. While concentrating on resolving the square, many callers ignored timing and smoothness completely. Many others were new enough to the square dance activity to have never been exposed to these skills at all. A memorized routine can be called so that each call arrives just as the dancers are completing the previous action. When this happens, the dancers can move into the next action without stopping. This is the goal of good timing. There is sometimes a problem when callers give the memorized calls too quickly. That's called "clipped" timing. It was common in the 1960's. Sight callers tend to have the opposite problem. Unless they are skilled at visualizing the dancer action before it is completed, they wait for the dancers to complete one call before they know what next call is possible. The hesitation of sometimes two, three or more beats of music results in stop-and-go dancing. That style of movement has become very common in modern square dancing.

## EXPERIMENTAL CALLS

The CALLERLAB dance programs and the quarterly selection (of experimental calls) program had been established in large part to stem the flood of new calls. The most experienced dancers had learned that almost all new calls disappeared forever as soon as the dance was over. For callers, on the other hand, the new call inserted into the favorite routines that they had learned provided an easy variety. The new calls didn't disappear quickly. But they did disappear. The way we all kept abreast of the new calls that were being created was to subscribe to note services. Some of the note services selected carefully from the horde of new calls. Jack Lasry's *Notes for Callers* was one of these. Jack selected one or two of the new calls each month and presented them with some choreography to show how to make the action danceable. Jack had been a teacher before he took up calling full-time and his note service offered many suggestions for improving the teaching of square dancing. The Santa Clara Valley Square Dance Callers Association, on the other hand, published a very popular note service with a very different philosophy. It was edited by Bill Davis. In the February 1984 issue, forty-four new calls were defined. In April 1994 only 12 new calls were described and Bill included the editorial observation that the supply of new calls had dwindled but that his service would continue to print any that were sent to him. In each issue some choreographic routines were included showing possible ways to use a few of the new calls. A page of Mainstream program material was also included. It showed unusual uses of calls CALLERLAB had chosen for particular emphasis during that quarter.

Another note service that intended to serve as a source of information about new calls as they were created was Bill Peters' *Choreo Breakdown*. In February 1984 he had only five new calls and in April, twelve. Don Beck took over *Choreo Breakdown* in 1985 and in February and April of 1988 had twenty-three and sixteen new calls respectively. (By 1989 Don's publication schedule had become somewhat irregular so I cannot compare the same five-year period.) Clearly the efforts of CALLERLAB a decade earlier had not stopped the flow of new calls. During the 1990's the creation of new calls did decline as Bill Davis noted in his April 1994 issue. By then the CALLERLAB dance programs had become accepted by nearly everyone and dancer interest in learning new calls focused mostly on the calls in the next program of dancing. Mainstream dancers wanted to learn Plus calls and Plus dancers wanted to learn Advanced program calls if they learned any call they didn't know. Learning something new that had no likely future use was not appealing - and probably never had been appealing. Possibly the dancers' apparent interest was because they were unable to tell which of the new calls they would be expected to know.

# CHAPTER 16 - PROBLEMS GET OUR ATTENTION

It took most of a decade for the reality of the trouble in the square dance world to become widely accepted. Hindsight shows us that convention and festival attendance began dropping in the early 1980's. That we didn't immediately recognize the shrinkage can be explained by a commitment to optimism; however, the fact that the numbers didn't shrink steadily helped us to ignore the message. While the peak attendance at the National Square Dance Convention came in 1983, it was a spike eight thousand people higher than the conventions before and after it. In fact the average attendance for the five years before 1983 and the five years that followed it were nearly the same at 23,063 and 22,431 respectively. A clear decline didn't become evident until the mid-1990's.

The New England Square Dance Convention reached its peak in 1977 but that information was not widely known. It was easy to blame the fluctuation in attendance numbers on the movement of the convention to a new location every two years. In New England, the Cooperation Committee made up of representatives of the dancers, callers and round dance leaders was responsible for the convention. Proceeds from the convention went to the organizations representing each of those groups. The Cooperation Committee seemed to be the only group concerned with low attendance and even they took several years to recognize the change. The number of clubs was still growing and attendance at club dances remained high through the 1980's.

Throughout most of the 1970's any group that offered square dance lessons in any reasonable population center could count on at least five squares signing up for the course which met weekly for twenty to thirty weeks. The survival rate from these classes into club members who came regularly to club events was low. But recruiting new class members had been easy enough to distract us from concerns about those who decided not to continue. My record keeping in the 1960's showed that about a quarter of those who started the class actually became regular dancers. That ratio certainly didn't improve. As we entered the 1980's, the first signs of trouble were beginning to appear. Recruiting was becoming more difficult. In the 1970's it wasn't unusual for a club to use the profits from their class to subsidize the club operations. A decade later it was more common for the club to spend from its treasury to support the classes. Club size stopped growing and so did the number of clubs.

It is very likely that recruiting of new square dancers reached a peak in the late 1970's. "Doc" Tirrell who edited *Grand Square*, the regional square dance magazine in Northern New Jersey, searched back issues to provide a count of total class size in that area year by year over the period 1968 to 1991. The numbers climb from 423 to a peak of 1021 in 1977 and then fall to less than 400 in 1990. I have no doubt that this schedule is representative of experience throughout North America.

## NEW ENGLAND SURVEY

Eventually a slowdown in class size did get attention from both clubs and callers. The New England Cooperation Committee, at a meeting in 1986, was presenting an attitude of gloom in a discussion of the recruiting problems that clubs were facing. I suggested that, in fact, we had no data that indicated whether square dancing was still growing or was shrinking. I pointed out that in the Manchester, New Hampshire area, for instance, where I had started my first club in 1956 it was common through most of the 1960's to have classes that were eight to ten squares of students. In 1986 that same area was being served by five clubs and the average class size was about two squares. My conclusion from this set of facts was that we were teaching the same number of people each year and that possibly our overall growth had not slowed. Rather, perhaps we had divided the square dance population into many clubs and were holding our own but distributing the available dancers over a much larger number of clubs. The result of this discussion was a survey supported by the Cooperation Committee. I began keeping an annual count of the actual number of dancers at weekend dances in New England during November. (We picked November because we felt that the folks with summer places would be back home and those who went south for the winter would not yet have left).

This annual survey collected actual attendance figures from as many club dances as we could for each Friday and Saturday in November. In order to provide some reasonable basis for comparison the results were presented as an average attendance at those dances for which I had all, or at least five consecutive, years of data. The number of dances that met this criteria climbed in the first five years to just over one hundred. The average attendance at those one hundred dances, starting in 1988 was 91 people. The averages for the next six years were 83, 84, 92 (in 1991), 86, 80 and 74 in 1994. The total number of different dances that were included in the 1988 survey was 211 and they were sponsored by 137 different clubs[18]. (Many clubs sponsored multiple weekend dances each month.) The average attendance at these 211 dances was 78. By 1994 the number of clubs responding to the survey had dropped to 120 and they reported on a total of 168 dances with an average attendance of 68 people. These are not hard numbers that can tell us the actual dancer population but they clearly show an unsurprising downward trend beginning somewhere in the late 1980's. They are also, to the best of my knowledge, the only record of actual attendance at club square dances over a region that has ever been collected.

The fact that the first couple of survey years didn't include any information about class size shows how slow we were to realize the most important cause of our problems. In 1988, Ed Juaire, who had taken over publication of the *Northeast Square Dancer Magazine*, suggested that we should start asking for information about classes. Thereafter we asked clubs to tell us whether they were sponsoring a class and, if so, how many students they had in the class. About half of the responding clubs report on their classes. The records show an average class size of twenty students shrinking to ten and a steady drop in the number of classes. The survey data document a steady drop of more than 60 percent in the number of people learning to square dance over the next decade.

## COULD DANCE PROGRAMS BE THE PROBLEM?

By the mid-1980's there were growing suggestions that the CALLERLAB standardized dance programs, now in place for a decade, were contributing

---

[18] The N.E. Directory in 1987 listed 152 clubs (all of which had to be members of EDSARDA) and 254 callers. Many of the clubs responding to my survey were not EDSARDA members and were not included in the Directory. (In N.E. nearly all the modern square dance callers belong to NECCA and thus are listed in the Directory.)

to and perhaps even causing the problems we were encountering. A press release issued by CALLERLAB in July of 1986 started:

> For the past year or more, the square dance world has been very concerned about the many problems that seem to be plaguing the activity - high drop-out rates, reduced festival crowds, club-to-class transition problems, etc. Groups of leaders such as CROSSFIRE and CROSSROADS have met to discuss these concerns and seek solutions. Out of all of these meetings has come the thought that the current CALLERLAB Mainstream Program of 68 families of basics, with a suggested 41 teaching sessions of 2 to 2 ½ hours each, may be longer than some areas can handle. An alternative entry level program that can be taught in 25 weeks has been widely suggested.

The meetings of leaders referred to in that release were organized by prominent dancers. CROSSROADS was held in Santa Monica, California and was mostly a group of committee heads for the 1988 National Square Dance Convention that was to be held in Anaheim, California. The CROSSFIRE meeting was held at Copecrest, a square dance resort formerly known as Andy's Trout Farm in Dillard, Georgia. After the 1985 CALLERLAB Convention, Jack Lasry had circulated a letter to many square dance leaders suggesting such a meeting. Jim White, a dancer and supplier of shoes to the square dance market, set about organizing the meeting. Jerry and Becky Cope donated the facilities of their resort as a place for caller and dancer leaders to convene and discuss the problems facing the activity. That these meetings were organized by dancers even though it was Jack Lasry who suggested them is an indication that dancer leaders recognized the growing problems well before the callers.

In fact it was only at meetings like this that the voice of the dancers could be heard. There was only one national organization that attempted to represent dancers. The United Square Dancers of America, Inc. (USDA) was formed in 1981 as a result of actions of the California Square Dance Council. They solicited participation from all the state organizations they could identify and received a good response. The first official meeting of this group took place in June during the 30th National Square Dance Convention in Seattle, Washington. The new group passed two motions of support. One was to support the California based National Folk Dance Committee that was attempting to get square dancing adopted as the United States' National Folk Dance. The other was support for another California-based committee, Square Dancers of America, whose goal was to present a square dance float each year in the Rose Bowl Parade. This was a time of success for modern square dancing and the new group did not reflect any recognition of problems.

I have always felt that the National Executive Committee (NEC), which is the self-perpetuating group that manages the National Square Dance Convention, has failed the square dance activity by not accepting a responsibility to represent dancers. The history of the USDA includes further comment on that subject. In 1983, the new organization approached the NEC requesting recognition at their conventions similar to that given to other square dance organizations like Legacy, CALLERLAB and ROUNDALAB. The response was an article in the magazine that the NEC published to promote their conventions that opposed the idea of a dancers' organization as not only unnecessary but perhaps even harmful to the activity. It is unfortunate that the NEC chose to protect their convention and was unwilling to accept any responsibility to contribute to the long-term success of square dancing.

USDA has continued to provide service to dancers. They eventually did win recognition by the National Square Dance Conventions and in the year 2001 USDA recognized fifty-three state, regional and area associations as full affiliates representing more than 100,000 dancers. The organization offers insurance, credit card, and prescription drug programs for their members and is involved in many promotional activities. They have shown an organizational interest in programs for youth, in schools and for handicapable people. One of their major activities has been an attempt to lobby the United States Congress to declare square dancing in all its forms to be the national dance. However, they have not seen it to be their responsibility to comment on the way dancing is presented by callers. Perhaps such a representation is not possible because square dancing is experienced in such a wide range of intricacy or format. Whatever the reason, the only awareness of how the customers feel about this activity is through the observation of callers.

The first half of the decade of the 1990's was a period of growing frustration for modern square dancing. In spite of continuing efforts to ignore the facts, it was becoming very clear that the activity had not only stopped growing, it was actually shrinking. Still, however, there was no generally accepted evidence. The facts were scattered and there were occasional successes and examples of growth. Everyone wanted to believe that we could return to the glory days of explosive growth. Nearly everyone who learned to square dance and became an active club member loved it. But classes were shrinking steadily and more and more clubs went out of business. *Sets in Order* magazine had shut down in 1985 but both *American SquareDance* and CALLERLAB's *Direction* newsletter contained many articles that either called attention to the growth problems or tried to explain them away as temporary or illusory. Gloom was spreading and the responsibility for the trouble was regularly assigned to the division of square dancers caused by the establishment of the programs of dancing by CALLERLAB.

CALLERLAB was not eager to accept responsibility or even to acknowledge the problems. The first organizational recognition of a recruiting problem happened in 1989 when the theme selected for the annual convention was RECRUIT, PROMOTE, MAINTAIN - RPM. The shrinking recruitment rate had finally gotten the attention of the callers. Dancers had become concerned earlier because they were the ones doing the recruiting. My response when the New England Cooperation Committee discussed the recruiting problem in 1986 was probably typical of the caller attitude. I attributed the smaller class sizes to the increased number of clubs. We didn't start collecting data on class size in the Co-op Committee survey until 1989.

The 1989 CALLERLAB Convention theme focused the attention of the caller community on the problems of both recruitment and retention, and the report was included in the June 1989 issue of *Direction*. Class schedules, marketing and advertising were all addressed. The report continued with a number of "consensus" statements. A few selections give a pretty clear picture of the thinking of the concerned leaders.- and more than 600 of them took part in the discussions.

> We are teaching dancers choreography, and not teaching them to socialize. We're teaching our people to be figure doers, not dancers. We're training the dancers to think if they are not learning something new, they should leave.

> We all need to work harder at the promotion of fun and fellowship and need to work toward the reduction of complexity.

> We should provide dances where new dancers can feel comfortable, and we must assist club members to accept new members and make them feel welcome.

> Need to work with your club dancers to help them be more receptive - kinder - to new dancers.

We should try to have classes the same night as club dances, thereby involving beginners immediately.

Of these points of agreement, the only one that had a real impact on the behavior of callers was the last and it was implemented primarily by the clubs for economic reasons. They could not afford to pay for the hall two nights and found they could pay for one night and teach the few students they had recruited without incurring additional expense. It is also true that callers were less expensive for one long night than they were for two separate nights.

The CALLERLAB Board of Governors gathered early at the 1992 Convention in Virginia Beach, Virginia to discuss the problems, their origin and possible solutions. A quote from my report of that meeting shows the thinking was not very different from the views expressed by the membership three years earlier.

About half the Board was able to arrive in Virginia Beach in time to take part in this session and, while we had only a couple of hours to devote to this session, some important observations come from it. There was nearly total agreement on the statements below. Following each one are a few quotes from the discussion to show how the participants were thinking about them.

Modern square dancing has become too complicated to allow effective recruitment of new participants.

Callers are too proficient.
There is a lot of bad judgment by callers.
Dancers are not bored. Callers are bored (or boring.)
Dancers don't judge difficulty, only their success.
Variety does not need to be difficult.
We are still promoting the ALL POSITION concept.
Widespread use of the MS & PLUS Standard Applications guidelines should help to make dancing easier.[19]

---

[19] The *Standard Applications* books published by CALLERLAB in 1991 are discussed later in this Chapter.

Modern square dancing has become too serious. We should promote the fun, sociability and the dancing experience more than choreographic skill at least in the MS & PLUS programs.

> People come together to be with other people.
> Let the people kick up their heels and have fun.
> At a one night stand people have fun. In class we regiment them too much.
> Add more variety by using different music.
> We haven't sold the dancing part of our activity.
> Callers need to be better entertainers.
> The different dance programs have separated friends.
> Callers should not encourage dancers to move to new programs.
> We should look for ways to promote mixing of dancers from all dance programs.

Along with these two main areas of agreement there were a couple of related thoughts about how CALLERLAB could help encourage easier dancing and more sociability.

> Our conventions should include presenters who can teach us to promote sociability and improve our entertainment skills.

> Both primary and continuing education for callers should include more emphasis on the importance of and how to achieve dancer success in all of our dance programs.

Against this background of concern in the United States, there were frequent reports of continuing growth in modern square dancing overseas. The message came from Germany, Scandinavia, Australia, New Zealand and Japan. Everywhere it was the same. The CALLERLAB programs work if they are used as they were intended. The programs are not a problem if dancers are really encouraged to stay in Mainstream dancing rather than being pushed to learn the Plus program. Teach the calls well and use them in many ways. All of these were strongly suggesting that we, the callers, had brought on our own problems. If we just followed our own advice, the problems would go away and square dancing would resume its growth in the United States just as it was growing everywhere else.

The Board of Governors' discussion did not accept the creation of dance programs as the basis for our difficulties. They did recognize that the programs divided the dancer population but the discussion put the blame for the problems facing modern square dancing on the complexity we had built in and the emphasis we were placing on choreographic skill. We knew that dancing had become very complicated and that it took a serious commitment to become a square dancer. But, in truth, many callers liked it that way and so did many of our customers, at least among those who had made the commitment and become regular dancers. Even the overseas callers who were being successful urged us to make dancers more proficient. They kept new dancers in class longer than was usual in the States and they kept them challenged both in class and later in the club with more intricate use of the Mainstream calls. A very popular view was that American dancers weren't willing to be "just Mainstream" dancers because they were bored. The callers who were most admired were the ones who could find the most unusual way to apply the definition of a call.

## MUSIC LICENSING

Traditional square dancing was nearly always done with an orchestra. It was done to traditional music. Few, if any, copyrights were involved and no one gave any thought to the matter of paying royalties to composers. A major factor in the growth of modern square dancing was the use of recorded music. The ability to have a dance without hiring an orchestra made it easy for small groups to hold a regular program of dancing. One of the changes that came with the modernization of square dancing was the use of popular music for the singing calls. We used all kinds of music from old folk songs to songs from Broadway musicals and jazz. As use of this music spread so did the number of companies producing records for square dancing. In the 1950's most of the record companies that were putting out music for square dancing were familiar with the copyright laws and they obtained the proper licenses for the commercial use of the music. For the record producer this is a license known as the mechanical license which is based on the number of records produced. Even the few small companies that ignored the need for the mechanical license put out such a small number of records that it wasn't worth the trouble to chase them. No one, however, gave any thought to the other license that is involved with the commercial use of copyrighted music, the performance license.

In 1990 all that changed. In the United States music performance royalties are primarily controlled by two major agencies, Broadcast Music Inc. (BMI) and American Society of Composers, Authors and Producers (ASCAP). Composers of music turn over the job of collecting payment for the performance use of their music to one of these agencies. The agencies issue licenses to radio and television stations and to theaters, dance halls and other places where music is regularly used for commercial purposes. Square dancing, however, was often, even usually, done in church and school halls and other places that were not regularly involved in the commercial use of music. They didn't have licenses. The dancers, however, were not exempt. They were using copyrighted music for commercial purposes. The fact that most of the clubs were nonprofit organizations did not relieve them from the obligation to pay for the music they used. The licensing agencies finally became aware of this illegal use of music. BMI got in touch with the publisher of the *National Square Dance Directory*, Gordon Goss, urging him to become a collection agent for the fees. He declined but they had a copy of the directory. They pressured Gordon to provide a computer-useable copy of his club listing. In the fall of 1990 on the advice of his lawyer he provided the list but limited it to one-time use. BMI used the list to send letters to the square dance clubs listed in the directory requesting that they obtain a license for their use of music.

The responsibility for providing a music license belongs by law to the sponsor of the event where the music is used. In square dancing this usually means that the club is the responsible group. The letters the clubs received made them aware of their responsibility for paying for the use of the music and offered a license for $15 per dance. Word spread rapidly in the square dance community. There were stories about agency representatives showing up at dances and threatening to shut the event down if the license fee wasn't paid. And there was a great deal of misunderstanding. Clubs and callers had been using whatever music they could get on a record for several decades without any thought about a legal obligation to pay for the right to use it. The idea that now they would have to pay didn't sit well. I was a member of the CALLERLAB Executive Committee in 1990 and I remember very clearly the discussions of this issue. Some said we should ignore it and it would go away. It took a great deal of education to make everyone understand that we had been ignoring a fully legitimate right of the music composer to be paid for his or her work. CALLERLAB and ROUNDALAB (the international association of round dance leaders) together concluded that asking clubs to pay a fee, even a $15 fee, for use of music at each dance would threaten the existence of many clubs that were struggling to make ends meet in a shrinking dance activity. We negotiated with BMI and ASCAP to allow the performer to be licensed instead of the sponsor of the event. This was a unique concept for them but we persuaded both the music associations that our activity was unique. They agreed to license callers and round dance teacher/cuers for an annual fee. Then the only obligation the club would have would be to assure that they used licensed leaders.

CALLERLAB had been formed as an invitation-only organization. To become a member a caller had to be invited to join. As we grew and our activities became more influential in the square dance world we set out to extend the invitation to every caller. Even so, full voting membership required that a caller attend an annual Convention at least once to qualify for membership and then once in every four years to maintain full membership. (For overseas members, that four years was extended to eight years.) The Board of Governors tried several times to persuade the membership to relax this requirement but that change was not to happen until 2001.

Liability insurance coverage was made available for our members. It was also offered to members of caller associations that affiliated with CALLERLAB. The music license was different. It was going to be necessary for every caller to be licensed. One of the conditions imposed by our agreement with the licensing agencies was that the license could be issued only to members and that every member who called in the United States would have to be licensed. In 1987 we had established Associate, Subscriber and Apprentice categories of membership. Of these, only the Associate included voting privilege. Our contracts with the music associations did not differentiate between forms of membership. They did, however, establish differences based on frequency of calling. This led to our establishment in 1991 of the Associate Licensee category for callers who did not meet the fifty-dance-per-year requirement to become Subscribers but were clearly not apprentices. One extension the contract did not allow was to offer the license to members of affiliated associations as we did with the insurance. The requirement to be licensed caused the membership of CALLERLAB to double in one year.

That requirement also created waves of resentment and misunderstanding. There were many who didn't accept the right of the music associations to control "our" music. They argued that the rules didn't apply to us since we didn't use the words of the original songs, at least not all of them. Others believed that CALLERLAB had invented the whole issue to increase our membership. The sessions that were set up at our 1991 Convention to answer questions about the licensing requirement drew overflow crowds and many of the participants were angry. One result of the resentment the licensing requirement generated was the formation of another caller association. Mac Letson a CALLERLAB member from Alabama, was offended by the effective forcing of all callers to join CALLERLAB. He and a couple of other callers formed the American Callers Association and arranged with the music agencies to provide the same licensing agreement to them which they were required to do by law.

# CHAPTER 17 - SOLUTIONS ARE PROPOSED

A lthough the dance programs were designed to change as the activity changed, there was a strong belief among callers that stability in the programs was important. CALLERLAB was reluctant to accept the idea that their dance programs were the cause of the troubles evident in the activity. But the pressure to consider that possibility was intense both from within the membership and from the dancers as expressed by their writing in the magazines. The idea of a complete revision of the dance programs was not welcomed enthusiastically but it had to be considered. The evidence was strong that new dancers were being rushed through the Mainstream program rapidly so they could dance at Plus program dances with the friends who had recruited them. There were also many who concluded that the length of the training period for new dancers was very long. They urged development of an entry program that would let new dancers dance at available dances. Such a program would include some, but not all, of the Plus calls.

## MAINSTREAM PROGRAM REVISION

In 1986, CALLERLAB established a new committee charged with the development of an entry program that could be taught in twenty-five weeks. The Mainstream Committee was also asked to review the calls on the Mainstream list and identify the most essential in bold type and italicize those less commonly used. The goal was to establish a group of calls that could be taught in twenty-five weeks, leaving the remainder to be taught in workshops after the twenty-five week class had ended. Both of these ideas had strong support and strong opposition among the CALLERLAB membership.

The committee charged with developing a new twenty-five week entry program was encouraged to include the most popular of the Plus calls and to eliminate Mainstream calls that were deemed less necessary. This was to be an entirely new program. Red Bates was appointed Chairman of that committee. For many years, Bill Davis, a caller from California, had been trying to persuade us that simply counting the frequency with which the calls were actually used would provide an adequate basis for establishing which calls should be taught first. Bill was a rocket scientist, literally, and his thinking often outstripped the ability of the rest of us to understand. Hardly anyone thought his system would work. There were a few of us who thought it was worth a try. Red Bates was one of these and he set about collecting tapes of dances from many callers representing many areas of the country. He did a count of the frequency of use of calls at these dances. That frequency count served as one of the major factors in the committee's creation of a proposed program of dancing that they believed could be taught in twenty-five weeks. The proposed program eliminated about ten of the primary calls then on the Mainstream program and included eight calls from the Plus program.

Consideration of both proposals for teaching square dancing in twenty-five weeks went on for a couple of years. The revised Mainstream list included a core set of calls in bold type that could be taught in twenty-five weeks with the remainder of the calls designated for addition later. The revised program proposed by the Red Bates committee also postponed teaching of many variations of the primary calls to reduce the teaching time. Both programs were presented to the membership of CALLERLAB in 1987. Both were accepted for trial periods. By the start of the 1990's, the status quo had triumphed and neither of the proposed program revisions was adopted.

## THE CALLERLAB FOUNDATION

While CALLERLAB didn't indicate any organizational recognition of the recruiting problem until the 1989 convention, several people had already expressed the view that we could make all of our problems go away with improved recruiting. They believed that better publicity would bring in more people. It was certainly true that square dancing was a well-kept secret. Dancers had always been so busy enjoying their dancing that they didn't spend much effort telling others about it. It seemed that we might interest more people in our activity if we could mount a big advertising campaign. While no organization had the money such an advertising campaign would take, one of the CALLERLAB members proposed a tax-exempt organization to preserve and promote square dancing. The idea came first from Bob "Fatback" Greene from Alabama whose daytime job was in the employ of the Cessna Aircraft Owners Association. He urged CALLERLAB to establish a foundation that could accept tax exempt donations and use the money to do a better job of publicizing square dancing. It seemed like a good idea. Square dancers were a loyal group who loved their activity and it was reasonable to assume that they would be willing to contribute to a promotional campaign with improved advertising. The initial legal work to establish the CALLERLAB Foundation was done by an Air Force buddy of Herb Egender who was then CALLERLAB's Assistant Executive Secretary. The Foundation was established in 1987 and a fund-raising campaign was initiated with Jerry Junck and Tim Marriner as chair and vice-chair. In October 1991 the initial campaign was closed with total contributions of nearly $90,000. Then Laurel Eddy found a lawyer in Georgia who took the next step to incorporate the Foundation and arrange United States Tax Exempt (501 c3) status for it. That became effective for donations made during and after 1991 and a new fund-raising campaign was announced.

The money donated, mostly by callers, in the initial campaign allowed the CALLERLAB Foundation for the Preservation and Promotion of Square Dancing to publish a full color, tri-fold brochure promoting the activity. The brochure was designed by CALLERLAB member Shawn Cuddy, a professional designer from Massachusetts, and featured the front page slogan "A <u>New</u> Song & Dance Routine." Inside the wording continued with "This is not your father's dance routine" which was a play on the Oldsmobile automobile advertising slogan "This is not your father's Oldsmobile." The initial distribution was without charge and more than 100,000 were distributed to callers and clubs all over the world in the first year. In order to avoid depletion of the Foundation assets the second and later printings were sold at cost. By the end of the 1990's nearly a million copies had been distributed.

## STANDARD APPLICATION BOOKS

A project that began in the late 1980's resulted in the 1991 publication of a book with the title *Standard Basic & Mainstream Applications*. The project had gathered input from a wide cross section of callers. Its objective was to identify the most common setups in which each of the Mainstream calls could be used. The project grew out of my experience as I started to call the

Advanced program in the early 1980's. I found that choreography I wrote didn't recognize the "usual" way that dancers encountered the calls. I wrote routines with problems like those that Clark Baker's computer-generated routines created. A call to Don Beck got me a list of the common setups for the calls on the Advanced list. From this experience I concluded that such a list might be helpful for less experienced callers as they began working with the Mainstream calls. The project was initiated with that goal in mind. The standard for inclusion in this publication was a reasonable expectation that most dancers (in the United States) would execute the calls successfully. One of the problems the committee working on the books encountered was how to describe the setups. Remember that the words formation and arrangement were not part of the common vocabulary of callers other than the caller coaches. Bill Peters who had chaired the Caller Training Committee when the Curriculum Guideline was published devised the final form of presentation. The page was divided into three columns. For each call in column one the formations that were standard were shown in column two and in column three the arrangements that were standard were shown for each of the standard formations.

This publication started a firestorm of confusion and confrontation between the advocates of easier dancing and those who favored more complicated choreography. The believers in choreographic challenge believed that this document would "dumb down" square dancing and become a standard for teaching. It also generated concern in square dance communities outside the United States. The Europeans, in particular, assured us that their dancers could easily handle a considerably wider variety of choreography. A second book was published a year later showing the comparable setups for the Plus program calls. When the committee proposed to extend this project to the Advanced program calls, there was strong resistance and that project was abandoned.

A comparison of the number of setups described as common in these books provides an interesting commentary on the state of square dance variety in the early 1990's. In the Basic program which included the first forty-nine calls on the Mainstream program, the number of variations considered standard for the calls averaged 4.4 per call. For the seventeen calls of the Mainstream program the number of standard setups dropped to an average of 3.9. In the Plus program the standard setups for the thirty-two calls in the program at that time averaged just over one per call. These are facts but there has been little attempt to interpret them. I have suggested a couple of interpretations to many of my peers. One is that the popularity of the Plus program is an attempt by the dancers to tell us they really don't enjoy choreographic variety as much as callers do. The other is that most of the variety in a Plus program dance will be produced by different uses of the Basic and Mainstream calls. Neither suggestion has found a warm reception among my caller friends.

The publication of the *Standard Applications* books focused more attention on the nature of choreographic difficulty. Throughout the 1980's there had been discussions among some callers about difficulty and dancer success but they were not widespread and attracted little interest. As noted in Chapter 14, when the Dance Level Identification Committee was developing the Plus program in 1977, I had a discussion with Lee Kopman about difficulty. We easily agreed that a vocabulary list of calls would not fully describe a dance level. We knew that full description would also require some way to grade the difficulty of the patterns. At that time the terms "formation" and "arrangement" as descriptors had not yet been accepted. Lee and I understood that very few callers had given any thought to the concept of identifying difficulty and we abandoned any further consideration of it. The *Standard Applications* books did, however, take a giant step toward identifying choreographic difficulty.

Many who objected to the idea of identifying standard and nonstandard choreography were concerned that this would provide a way to further divide the existing dance programs. They foresaw "standard" Mainstream dances and "nonstandard" Mainstream dances. For each of the program vocabularies there would now be a standard way of using the calls and "another" way. That was never the intent of the books but it took a substantial education program over the next five years to bring about understanding of the purpose for their publication.

Perhaps the books did help to generate the extensive discussion of choreographic difficulty and dancer success that was a part of CALLERLAB conventions during the first half of the 1990's. As a member of the Executive Committee I may have contributed more than my share to programming of convention sessions with subjects like these in 1991:

Making Routine Fun, KISS - Keep It Successfully Simple and Degree of Difficulty,

And these in 1992 when the convention theme was Success By Design: Controlling Difficulty, Formation Management, and KISS (again)

The 1993 Convention in Louisville, Kentucky had as a theme "Improving the Dance Experience" and the program paid attention not only to the matter of difficulty and dancer success but also included several sessions about the style aspects of dancing. The list of session titles and presenters shown here indicates an unprecedented attention to the non-choreographic components of square dancing.

I - Successful Choreo; Oxendine, Junck, Bronc Wise, O'Leary
II - Smoothness in Dancing; Beck, Cuddy, Reed, Morvent
III - Timing & Phrasing; Kaltenthaler, Deck, Leger
IV - Working with Music; Berg, Driver, Sheffield, Perry
V - Leadership Solutions; Kinney, Wayne McDonald, Jim Wheeler
VI - Showmanship; Oxendine, Dougherty, Murray, Story
VII - Formation Management; Kaltenthaler, Jacobs, Stevens
VIII - One Night Stands; Anderson, Aubut, Burdick
IX - Degree of Difficulty; Sybalsky, Jacobs, Reese

By 1995 Jerry Reed, the chairman of the Choreographic Applications Committee that was custodian of the *Standard Applications* books, was asked to make a speech to the convention to assure that everyone understood their original purpose. He explained that the intention behind publication of the books was to allow new callers to understand what uses of the calls were likely to cause dancers difficulty. In 1996, the Board of Governors approved a policy statement about the books and the membership voted overwhelming approval of the policy. With these words it declared the end of the use of the terms All Position Dancing and Dance By Definition:

For every square dance move, certain setup situations are used more frequently than others. These setups, or "applications" of the moves are those the dancers hear most often and thus these applications are most familiar to the dancers, and provide the lowest level of difficulty.

Callers and dancers have learned that choreographic sequences using only the most familiar formations and arrangements (of men and women) for each move are easier to dance than sequences containing less familiar applications. CALLERLAB encourages callers to manage the difficulty of the dance routines they use to assure a high degree of dancer success.

Over the past several years CALLERLAB research has identified which applications are used most often. The name given to these most common formations and arrangements is Standard Applications. These are defined as "Those formations and arrangements from which a move may be called with nearly 100% success at an open dance or festival."

The Standard Applications for Mainstream and Plus moves have been identified and published in two books. These Standard Application books provide callers a way of knowing what dance patterns will allow dancers to be successful most of the time at open dances and festivals. Callers then also know that when extended applications of movements are used, a lower success rate may result.

Although CALLERLAB is aware that the use of some extended applications which are not standard is a valuable programming tool, but callers should pay close attention to the dancer success rate. Callers using extended applications are encouraged to be prepared to provide extra help to the dancers as needed to assure adequate success. Dancer enjoyment of such choreography depends heavily on the caller's ability to provide just the right mix of challenge and success.

Future CALLERLAB documents will use the term "Standard" to identify choreography using those applications which are most familiar to the dancers. The term "extended" will be used by CALLERLAB to identify choreography which is less familiar to dancers, i.e. those applications not listed in the Standard Applications books.

Identification and publication of the Standard Applications effectively replaces the concepts of "All Position Dancing" (APD) and "Dance By Definition" (DBD). These terms were never clearly understood and CALLERLAB suggests that they are no longer needed to identify what may now be described as extended choreographic dance applications.

## MEMBERSHIP SURVEY

The debate within CALLERLAB over the possibility that the troubles in modern square dancing could be traced to the dance programs continued throughout the early 1990's. The Executive Committee decided that it was important for the organization to know as accurately as possible how the membership felt about this question. They commissioned a commercial public opinion research firm, S.T.A.R.S., Inc. of Ann Arbor, Michigan to design a survey questionnaire that would determine how the members felt about the dance programs. It was a detailed survey sent to a statistically representative sample of the membership and the sixty-five percent response rate showed a high level of commitment and concern. The responses were analyzed to indicate both the overall attitudes and a breakdown of the differences among subgroups like traveling callers, local club callers, overseas members, callers of the advanced programs and many others.

The results were reported in the December 1993 issue of *Direction*. Detailed analysis of the responses showed clearly that callers were not of one mind with regard to the content of the dance programs. There were no major variations based on frequency of calling, geographic location or calling experience. While there was strong support for the concept of worldwide program acceptance, there was substantial ambivalence with respect to what calls should be included in those programs and how the calls should be apportioned between them. That division of opinion was to be expressed even more convincingly in a few more years.

## T - 2000

At the 1996 convention in Kansas City, Missouri, pressure to consider the possibility that CALLERLAB Programs were the cause of the problems in modern square dancing came to a head. A debate was scheduled and it was announced in the convention program:

Alternate Dance Programs - a Debate, Seastrom, Story (Pro), Jones (Con)

In the early days of CALLERLAB, many issues were resolved by presenting several viewpoints for membership consideration. For many years there have been private debates within our membership about the impact of our dance programs on the success of square dancing. The debate in this year's convention program returns to that earlier format, presenting both sides of a proposal to restructure the CALLERLAB square dance programs. A proposed change would eliminate the Plus Program by moving the entire Plus Program into a unified Advanced Program. The Advanced Program would be consolidated into a single program combining all the present Plus calls and the present A-1 and A-2 calls. The debate will not focus on the details of the proposed change. Rather it will consider whether a change like this would have a positive effect on square dancing in the long run. The debaters for both sides feel strongly about this issue and the program promises to set you thinking about your own views. There will be adequate time following the debate for a question and answer period.

During the debate Jon Jones presented the case for staying with the existing programs and against an alternative program structure. As the discussion from the floor was drawing to a close, Jon let the group know that he had been asked to take that side of the debate and acknowledged that he, personally, believed the existing structure was not working. His exact words were "My own personal feeling is that we should adopt a program that can be taught in no more than twenty weeks and eliminate everything else."

Discussion from the floor following the debate culminated in a consensus that a committee should be formed to study alternative dance programs. Tony Oxendine, then CALLERLAB Chairman, was in attendance at this session and established an ad hoc committee on the spot. Jerry Story and Jon Jones were named as Chair and Vice Chair. The June issue of *Direction* invited anyone interested in joining this committee to contact the chairman. The Committee was charged to consider whether an alternative structure of dance programs should be developed. If the answer was yes, they were to present an alternative structure proposal to the Board. They tackled the job with enthusiasm. Many of those who had attended the debate in Kansas City signed on to the committee.

In 1997 the committee met at the convention in Los Angeles and recommended a new program structure. The Board of Governors decided that a change of this magnitude required the widest possible consideration. They agreed that the proposal would be presented for final acceptance or rejection at the 1998 Convention near Cincinnati, Ohio. A committee was formed, again headed by Story and Jones, to give the proposal the widest possible exposure. They were called the Team 2000 and the team included all the members of the Executive Committee and some of the Program Committee Chairs.

The next year was one of nearly continuous debate. Each issue of *Direction* included articles in support of and opposed to the new proposal. Many of us on Team 2000 wrote articles on both sides of the question to assure the widest possible presentation of all the issues involved. A MiniLab[20] was held in Portland, Maine in September 1997 - the first held within the United States - and it provided an opportunity for open, face-to-face discussion of the issues. It was a hot issue with strong feelings on both sides. The debate was intense but polite.

With some small modification made by Team 2000, the following proposal was presented to the CALLERLAB membership at the 1998 Convention for acceptance or rejection in its entirety.

(1) The proposed first dance program shall contain calls from the existing Basic Program that can be readily taught in 12 sessions, each session being two hours in duration, from Standard Applications only; and

(2) The proposed second dance program shall contain calls that are currently listed in the existing Mainstream and Plus Programs or calls from the Basic Program that were not selected for inclusion in the proposed first dance program, if any, that can be readily taught from Standard Applications in 12 additional two-hour sessions; and

(3) The proposed third dance program shall contain the Extended Applications of all calls listed in the proposed first two dance programs. This proposed third dance program could be taught in no less than 25 additional two-hour sessions.

Most of that Convention was devoted to continued explanation of the proposal and discussion of it. The four hundred and seventy-five people at that convention reversed a six-year downward trend in convention attendance. It was also the first time in six years that more than 20 percent of the CALLERLAB membership attended a convention. The outcome was at once a shock and a clear statement of the division within the leadership of modern square dancing. The motion failed to pass on a tie vote in a written ballot of 116 to 116.

---

[20] MiniLabs were established by CALLERLAB to provide a way for members from outside North America to satisfy the meeting attendance requirements without incurring major travel costs. The previous MiniLabs had been held in England and Australia. The Portland MiniLab was an attempt to find out whether the concept applied in North America would encourage wider membership.

## PHOENIX PLAN

In 1999 Mike Seastrom brought a guest to the convention in Dallas, Texas to speak to the Board of Governors. Jim Hensley had recently learned to dance in one of Mike's classes and he also ran a public relations company. Jim was hooked on square dancing and he saw it as the world's greatest recreational product. He also saw it as one of the best-kept secrets he had ever encountered. He was a persuasive speaker and an island of positive thinking in a sea of gloom. The Board asked him to give a condensed version of his talk to the membership at the opening meeting and he was equally persuasive with this group. His basic message was that we had an absolutely marvelous activity that a recreation-starved population desperately needed. If we would only let the world know that we existed, Jim was quite sure that we could fill our halls again. Jim was in the public relations business and urged us to come together, both callers and dancers, to raise enough money to let the world know we were there. He was quite sure that we would find both government and corporate support readily available.

It had been clear to everyone for some time that telling the world about our activity would cost money and the Foundation Fund Raising Committee had come up with an idea. During the Dallas Convention eleven of our best-known callers got together to record a square dance version of the song *"God Bless the USA."* At the closing banquet they performed the song live and raised the spirits of the group to an unprecedented level. A limited edition of the recording, 200 numbered copies made on white vinyl, was sold at premium prices and the number one and number 200 copies were auctioned at the banquet. More than $10,000 was raised that night to kick-off a fund-raising campaign to finance a new level of promotion for square dancing. The rest of the record run was sold, along with tape copies, to dancers and callers who had not attended the convention. Contributors were told that the funds would be used for a "real" program to promote square dancing and the fund grew to more than $60,000 within a couple of years.

Jim Hensley was appointed Marketing Advisor for the Foundation. He was generous with his time but he did ask for, and was given, reimbursement of his firm's expenses as he guided us in the early stages of marketing our product. He also set about trying to enlist support from the dancer community. He came up with a long-range plan for the rebirth of modern square dancing. He and we came up with the name The Phoenix Plan obviously hoping that we could rise again from the ashes all about us. He was convinced, and tried to make us understand, that any large scale approach to governments or corporations for support would require us to show that we had a united community that could work together to promote our activity. The wide support for our fund-raising was encouraging. One of the early steps included in the Phoenix Plan was some market research. Jim tried several firms and settled on the same firm that had done our 1993 survey, now operating as StarWorks, Inc., as the company to do the research.

The first step was a survey conducted on the Internet which allowed questions to be asked of a group of people demographically representative of the United States population for a reasonable cost. That survey determined that a bit less than 20 percent of the population had some contact with square dancing as adults. We also learned that our public image was not as bad as we had imagined and that nearly everyone who had actually tried square dancing was enthusiastic about it. Based on that result we then sponsored a series of focus-group research efforts to further understand the public attitude toward our product. These were conducted in three cities, Charlotte, South Carolina, St. Louis, Missouri and Portland, Oregon. Three focus groups were set up in each city with participants selected to represent the 35 to 55 age group that many of us felt was most likely to be customers for our product. We recognized that the learning process demanded a significant commitment of time and thus we felt that people whose children were, or soon would be, leaving home would be our most likely candidates.

The results of this program of market research were reported at the 2001 Convention in St. Louis, Missouri and a full report was sent to the major contributors who supported the research. These included The National Executive Committee, The 42nd National Convention which was held in St. Louis in 1993, Grand Square, Inc. a charitable foundation headquartered in Charlotte, North Carolina and Andy Shore who is a CALLERLAB member from California. The report was also made available to anyone who requested it.

The report of this research contained few surprises. We were told that our target age group was very busy, not inclined to make commitments and regarded square dancing as an activity for older people, if they knew of it at all. Most people were unaware that square dancing was available in their community although all three of the locations had many active clubs. The common image of square dancing was of the traditional form and the people in our focus groups knew nothing of square dance classes or clubs. It is clear that our promotional efforts have been unsuccessful. When asked if they might be interested in an activity such as ours most of the participants found the commitment required to be unappealing.

The executive summary by StarWorks, Inc. ended with some suggestions. These included creation of a diverse set of program offerings (referring particularly to the absence of programs for dancers unwilling to commit to the long class cycle.) The summary also recommended collaboration between clubs in a city or region and between callers and clubs. Relaxation of some club norms and more active promotion and marketing were also recommended. These recommendations came in part from additional focus groups of former dancers - we call them "dropouts" - in St. Louis and Portland. Their discussions provided insight into what caused folks to leave the activity. It also made it clear that even though these people were no longer dancing their view of the square dance experience is strongly positive. People who try it like it even when politics, excessive time commitments and inter-club or intra-club squabbling cause them to give it up.

# CHAPTER 18 - THE NEW MILLENNIUM ARRIVES - WHERE ARE WE?

As we entered the new millennium, nearly everyone involved realized that modern square dancing was in serious trouble. The Foundation fund-raising effort had faded before enough money was raised to continue the marketing effort beyond the research. Jim Hensley had discovered, and made us face, that the community was not united. Each of the organizations in modern square dancing was wary, at best, of the other organizations. With encouragement from Jim Hensley, CALLERLAB has tried in several ways to build a modern square dance community that includes representatives of the dancer organizations in addition to the caller and round dance leader organizations. We have reached outside the square dance community to establish cooperation with the National Dance Association, an organization interested in promoting all forms of dance. While there are signs of growing trust and cooperation, we still have a long way to go.

The book *Bowling Alone: The Collapse and Revival of American Community*, by Robert Putnam was published in New York by Simon & Schuster in 2000. For me, personally, reading it was a revelation. The book describes modifications in our society that have taken place over the past fifty years. These changes explain the experience of the square dance activity in a way that has nothing, or at least very little, to do with the way that modern square dancing has developed over that same period. Dr. Putnam shows with extensive research data that a wide range of activities requiring participation has followed a pattern of growth and decline during the last fifty years that is almost exactly the same as modern square dancing.

189

His conclusion is that, for reasons not fully explained by his research, the number of people who join organizations of any kind that require participation has decreased, generation by generation, from those that fought World War II to less than half in the generation that is now entering college.

There had been earlier mentions of Dr. Putnam's ideas. In 1996, Freddie Kaltenthaler wife of John the former Executive Director of CALLERLAB, wrote a review in *Direction* of an article by Dr. Putnam presenting the same thesis. A detailed report of another article by Dr. Putnam on the same subject was reprinted in the June 1997 issue of Direction. Many of us failed to realize the implication of these early references. In the mid-1990's we were not ready to see that the decline in our recruiting might be caused by something other than our lack of promotion or the failure to manage our dancing programs.

I wrote a book report of *Bowling Alone* that was published in the August 2000 issue of *Direction*. A few paragraphs from that report describe the change in my understanding of our situation that came from reading the book:

> Social capital is the central topic of a book published early in the year 2000. The book, *Bowling Alone*, was written by Robert D. Putnam who is a Professor of Public Policy at Harvard University. The core idea of social capital is that social networks have value. Physical capital is the facilities and equipment that improve productivity. Human capital is the education and training that make people more effective. Social capital has that same kind of value. It refers to the "connections among individuals - social networks and the norms of reciprocity and trustworthiness that arise from them." Strong connections and trust allow people to resolve collective problems more easily. Social capital also "greases the wheels that allow communities to advance smoothly. Where people are trusting and trustworthy—everyday business and social transactions are less costly."

> Reading this book has made a very substantial impact on my thinking about the past and the future of modern western square dancing - and perhaps of traditional square dancing as well. I have worked and studied for at least two decades to try to understand how the changes that we have made caused the decline in participation. This book has made clear to me that our changes had a very moderate impact on our ability to maintain the popularity of

our activity. The bulk of the decline resulted from the generational differences and a general decline in participation in groups such as ours. I have now given up trying to find out what we did wrong - and trying to fix it in the hope that the fix will restore the popularity we once had. I now understand that the challenge facing us is to find ways to compete more effectively in a shrinking marketplace. We may also have to learn from past mistakes but without the sense that they have caused the problems we face.

Professor Putnam does not leave us without suggesting a course of action to correct what he believes is a serious deficiency in our society. He suggests several goals for the next decade. Some of them fall within the reach of our activity. He asks us to find ways to increase the access to social capital for those coming of age during the next ten years. Making square dancing more successful could be a huge step toward that goal. He urges us to "find ways to ensure that by 2010 Americans will spend less leisure time sitting passively alone in front of glowing screens and more time in active communication with our fellow citizens." Square dancing is a wonderful alternative leisure time recreation with no glowing screens in sight. Finally he urges "Let us find ways to ensure that by 2010 significantly more Americans will participate in (not merely consume or 'appreciate') cultural activities from group dancing to songfests to community theater to rap festivals." Clearly we have a common interest.

We have known - even before we knew the term - that square dancing is a wonderful way to build social capital. It brings together people from all walks of life into a cooperative, usually community-based group. We have all seen the strength of the sense of belonging and genuine lifelong friendships that are created in square dancing. We now have an advocate to tell us with overwhelming evidence how important are these contributions to the health and strength of our society. Square dancing is not only fun, it is also a valuable gift that we can give to all who take part and to the communities where we live. Let us redouble our efforts to make the joy we know available to our neighbors.

While I, personally, concluded that our experience of decline in modern square dancing was only slightly the result of changes we had made, most others continued to search for a way to "fix" square dancing. I also believed that the complex activity we had created was not likely to be a mass-appeal product in a market environment where people wanted less commitment. Modern square dancing today requires at least a hundred nights of dancing in the first couple of years before a new recruit can expect to be comfortable as a competent dancer. The focus group research had made it clear that the group we identified as most likely to be potential customers for our product was not at all interested in making that kind of commitment.

Among the leaders within CALLERLAB, the message is being heard reluctantly. There is a growing awareness that the future of the activity we have created, known and loved is at risk of shrinking into oblivion. No one expects that it will go away completely. There are still strong programs and clubs outside the United States although it is likely that even these are just a decade or so behind us on the same path. The enthusiasm for more dancing complexity is even stronger in those areas than it is here. There are some young people entering the modern square dance activity. There are a few growing clubs even here in the U.S.

One of the changes that seems to be working is called the multi-cycle class. One of our most obvious problems is that throughout the life of modern square dancing it has been possible to join a new class only in the fall. The length of time it took to learn the basic vocabulary reached more than half a year sometime in the early 1960's. Since then, classes have nearly all begun in the fall and continued for a full dance season. The multi-cycle approach starts new dancers every ten to fifteen weeks. The teaching time is shortened so that two and sometimes three of these groups meet on the same night in the same hall blending the boundary between groups. One advantage this approach offers is that people who are not comfortable with what they have learned so far can easily repeat the cycle they have just completed on the same night and without interrupting the dancing experience. They can even decide that they don't want all the complexity that modern square dancing has to offer and can keep coming only to the first group.

The Executive Committee of CALLERLAB, while brainstorming after a meeting in 2001, agreed that it could try to promote a much easier form of modern square dancing without interfering with the effort to rebuild the existing form of the activity. This was a giant step toward a new way of thinking. One direct result of this change was active support of a program for teaching callers how to do a better job of calling for non-dancers who were not in class. The Community Dance Program (CDP) that CALLERLAB invented in 1987 was an initial attempt to build a program based on a very limited set of calls. The CDP Committee, under the chairmanship of Cal Campbell, tried diligently and demonstrated to their own satisfaction by late in the 1990's that the concept didn't sell well. My personal view, with the benefit of hindsight, is that a possible reason for the failure of the Community Dance Program was that it did not retain the instantaneous changing choreography that is the unique characteristic of modern square dancing. As a program that looked a lot like traditional square dancing it was not welcomed by modern callers.

There have been presentations at several recent conventions showing how to do a good job with parties for folks who have not had square dance training. There are several CALLERLAB members serving an active market among people who are not involved in clubs. Jerry Helt of Cincinnati Ohio and Bob Howell, also from Ohio, have been very successful in that market for several decades. Gregg Anderson in Colorado Springs gave up calling for clubs a few years ago in favor of more involvement with the non-club square dance activity. He has been very successful. There is no question that square dancing, along with the related round and line dance forms, is a very marketable product for a one-night party. The difficulty arises when we try to convert these one-nighters into repeating customers who will come back week after week. Unless there is a change in our society or in our product it is not clear that we will be successful in that endeavor.

# CHAPTER 19 - A SUBJECTIVE SUMMARY

Throughout this book I have done my best to be objective. Keeping my own prejudice and opinions under control has not been easy. As a leader in the caller community for more than four decades, I feel I must accept part of the responsibility for what modern square dancing has become. This chapter will consider how we might have done things better. I have strong opinions about what we have done right and mistakes we have made. While the facts in *Bowling Alone* suggest much of what happened would have occurred no matter what we did, it is clear to me that had we done some things differently, we might be in a better position to compete for customers even in today's society.

We have a wonderful recreational product. Our problem is tunnel vision. We seem only to be able to envision it as it is - at the moment. Even the way square dancing was in its most successful time seems to hold little interest for those who are still dancing or calling. Most of them have been involved for more than a decade. People have adapted to the changes - or they are gone. Modern square dancing is the creation of a particular generation of people. They were born between 1915 and 1940. Beginning in 1950 they changed an activity that had always depended on the dancers learning a routine to one with changing routines that dancers could not anticipate. Perhaps this happened because improved sound equipment made it possible for the dancers to hear and respond to changes made while the dance was happening. Certainly improved equipment made it more possible to dance to records. A live musician was no longer necessary for a square dance. Perhaps it was just that the excitement of changing choreography was well suited to the temperament of this generation.

The dance routine that changed as it was being danced provided the basis for a very different form of square dancing. Instead of learning a dozen routines that were done the same way at every dance, the dancers learned a set of calls which were used in different ways every time they danced. In the beginning, the number of calls that had to be learned was small, no more than twenty. When a dance routine included something the dancers had not seen before, they were shown how to do it - they were "walked through" - before the caller started the dance. Callers had to learn new routines but dancers did not. There was great choreographic variety even with our limited set of calls. The heritage of live music was still with us, too. We danced to the music. Choreographic routines - particularly singing calls - were developed in multiples of eight beats so that they fit the phrase of our music which was - and still is - nearly all written in eight beat phrases[21]. The adaptation of square dance routines to modern songs became very common.

During the first decade (1950 - 1960) a few new calls were added to the language of modern square dancing. The most durable of these were Square Thru and Wheel and Deal. The vocabulary grew slowly because every new call added a memorization load to the caller's task. In the next decade we developed ways to add new calls into our choreography without needing to memorize new routines. Sight, modules and mental image methods allowed us to fit the new calls into our memorized routines. By 1970 we had created more than four thousand new calls. A few of them stayed around and became part of the vocabulary a new dancer had to learn. In that decade the usual class time for a new dancer grew from fewer than ten sessions to more than twenty. Where we had been running two classes each year we could now fit in only one.

In that same decade we began to develop a dancing elite group. For them modern square dancing was more of a hobby than just a social recreation. Many of the people who joined our classes accepted the need for the time in class so they could join in a once-a-week or twice-a-month activity that brought them together with other people from their community. They didn't

---

[21] In New England the quadrille heritage led to dancing that allowed the dancers to start most actions on the first beat of the musical phrase. In the Southeast and West it was more common for the caller to fit his (and occasionally, her) call words to the phrase thus making the dancers' connection to the musical phrase much less important. But everyone danced to the beat taking their steps in time with the rhythm of the music.

come to learn skills that could be constantly improved. They just wanted to be part of the group. Many others found in the first few weeks of class an activity that offered different levels of accomplishment. Modern square dancing has been nearly paranoid about avoiding anything that could be called competition, but it is clear on the first night of a class that some dancers are more skilled than others. The speed with which the better dancers identify each other and join together in set squares is astounding.

The tendency for better dancers to come together may also explain why the leadership in most square dance clubs comes from that more eager group. Whatever the explanation, it is certainly true that club officers usually come from the most active group of dancers. They are likely to be the ones who dance at the front of the hall and are more likely to dance in successful squares. One of the early mistakes that I believe I made may be a fundamental explanation for the state of modern square dancing today. After the first three years of calling for the first club I had started the officers came to me with a request that I make the dancing more challenging. They had traveled to other groups and danced to different callers and they wanted to be prepared to dance successfully in those situations. I did what they asked. We extended the length of class from the five lessons we had started with to ten. I taught a few more calls and started to use more complicated routines. I believe that was a mistake. I should have encouraged them to start a new group for those who wanted that kind of dancing while keeping the original club the same as it had been.

Another illustration of the impact of the experienced, eager dancer on the evolution of modern square dancing is the encouragement they gave to callers to make the dancing challenging. Anyone who was calling during the twenty years that started in the mid-1960's will remember what it took to win a reputation as a great caller. That was to call so the dancers at the front of the hall were challenged - and at least sometimes broken down - no matter what that did to the squares at the back of the hall. The dancer/caller interaction was seen by both as a competition. Better callers were the ones who could call routines that the dancers couldn't handle. As we have noted, dancers never blamed the caller for the breakdowns in their squares. The accepted view was that if the dancers were only more skilled they could have succeeded. This attitude led to competition among callers to find more intricate dance routines or, during the 1960's, a newer call to teach. The caller that got hired back was the one that broke down the floor. The callers who called routines that everyone could do successfully got less work.

This attitude of competition to call more intricate dance routines is a core element of modern square dancing. It is accepted today by the majority of callers and dancer leaders. No matter how much we give lip service to - or even serious concern for - the importance of dancer success, the appeal of the more "interesting" choreography is ever present. Very few callers include the quality of the dancing experience in their evaluation of choreography. Whether the action flows smoothly or can be accomplished by most of the dancers without major hesitations is of little importance. Dancer breakdowns are little noticed by a large share of sight callers who must watch a successful square in order to follow the action in their own minds. Even callers committed to the importance of dancer success don't notice the breakdowns when they are working with unusual choreography they have not yet memorized.

Clark Baker has been working for several years on a revision of the Mainstream definitions that will allow extensions of them in ways that were never imagined twenty years ago. As just a small illustration of this consider the call Circle to a Line. In the 1960's this call was used only following a direction to Head or Side couples to lead right. Clark is now considering questions about whether the call can be used from facing lines or with two boys facing two girls. Some want to know whether a direction of rotation is established for any of the dancers at the end of the call so that a call to Roll could be used next. In many areas the dancers have created their own variation of this action that is quite different from the official action no matter how it is described. A major force for the definition precision has come from Europe. Callers there have been looking for ever more unusual ways to use the existing calls - and chiding those in the States for using the calls only in fairly standard ways.

Since the early 1990's there has been a growing recognition that an activity in which half of the participants are expected to fail frequently has a less-than-universal appeal. And this is the gentlest way I can describe modern square dancing. The acceptance of this, to me, self-evident truth is not yet widespread among the leadership of both callers and dancers. The belief that dancers are at serious risk of boredom is widespread. Callers share with each other bits of unusual and intricate choreography. Rarely do they concern themselves with the smoothness or danceability of the material they are sharing. Caller schools still concentrate on teaching callers to provide choreographic variety.

I have believed throughout my square dance life that before I can object to the way things are, I must demonstrate the viability of my proposed alternative. I have been unable to do this. There may be others who have but I don't know of any. There are continuing square dance programs based on a limited set of calls but they are not filled with young, able-bodied people. They are senior groups or groups with physically or mentally challenged people. I do not know of any successful group that meets as often as once a month and does modern square dancing with a program based on less than the Mainstream list of calls. Several attempts have been made to create and maintain such a group. They have failed. The CALLERLAB Community Dance Program was based on the assumption that such groups were both viable and needed. It was never successful.

Why, then, am I enthusiastic about the potential for such a program? Perhaps it is because I remember the pleasure I experienced dancing in the early days of modern square dancing. I have also learned much about my own enjoyment of square dancing today as I have tried to understand my current dancing experiences. I am reluctant to dance much now because good dancing experiences - as I define them - are not readily available. Even when I find a caller able to let me dance smoothly to the music with choreography that everyone in my square can accomplish, it is uncommon to find a square of people who will dance with style and grace. When I do find that wonderful combination, I have learned that I am totally unaware of the dance program or the intricacy of the choreography. The dancing is fun.

If I enjoy it, there must be others. The kind of dancing I enjoy doesn't depend on a large vocabulary of calls. It does depend on changing choreography. It also depends on dancers who have been taught how to dance. Modern square dancing has sacrificed dancing to the pursuit of choreographic innovation. It is a death spiral. The classes we teach effectively separate from the general population only those who are willing to learn endlessly. In class we let them win, mostly, but when they finish class they must also be willing to spend a year in which there is a high level of failure. Few who have survived this initiation want to see it changed. Any group that tries to offer a slower or less challenging introduction to modern square dancing finds their most skilled customers lured away by raiders from other groups.

It may be necessary for the existing program to fade completely before a different form of modern square dancing can exist. Perhaps the generation of people who enjoy what we have created will be replicated at some time in the future. There don't seem to be many among those who are less than sixty years old now who are willing to make the commitment it takes to become a modern square dancer. I know we can easily offer an activity that would provide most of the recreational value of modern square dancing with much less commitment. We can make square dancing fun with any size vocabulary of calls. The social value of club membership, which is a critical component of the enjoyment most have found in modern square dancing, is not dependent on vocabulary size. The primary deterrent to creation of such a new form is the inflexibility of the existing participants. As soon as most callers find a group of people, they start to stretch their choreographic skills - even on the first night of class. As soon as many dancers encounter a new recruit they encourage them to move with all possible haste to a program of dancing beyond their ability.

There are, even now, success stories. Several clubs have been experimenting with the multi-cycle approach. This allows new people to be brought into the activity three or four times each year instead of the past practice of starting classes only in the fall. It also makes a much more socially comfortable situation for people who want a less committed level of involvement. Many of these experiments have reversed the trend toward shrinking clubs. These clubs are growing. They are learning that people in new dancer groups (the word "class" has been abandoned) that are having a good time are the best recruiters. The size of the entry groups is growing. These methods work best when the club leaders and the caller are willing to give up - or at least, lessen - their fascination with complicated choreography. The goal of choreographic variety remains but, unless the dancers succeed, the variety loses its appeal. The successful clubs also slow the pace of learning. There is more emphasis on enjoyment of the dancing and less on adding new calls to the vocabulary.

My definition of good square dancing is to move smoothly to the music through changing dance routines that we can accomplish successfully in the company of friends who share and participate in our pleasure. That describes the modern square dance that I have loved for fifty years. The "moving smoothly" and "accomplish successfully" have been in short supply for the last couple of decades. I hope that we can revive them and use them to rebuild a wonderful recreation.

# BIBLIOGRAPHY

Beck, Don, *Out of Sight*, Stow, Massachusetts, Published by the author, 1983

Bell, Don & Dawson, Bob, *The Keys to Calling Square Dances*, Florida, published by the authors, 1961.

Brown, Jack & Sue, *Steps in Time*, Dallas, Texas: North Texas Square and Round Dance Association, 1985.

Burdick, Stan, *The Windmill System of Hash Calling*, Sandusky, Ohio, published by the author, 1965.

Burleson, Bill, *The Square Dancing Encyclopedia*, Minerva, Ohio, published with periodic updates by the author, 1970.

*CALLERLAB Curriculum Guidelines for Caller Training & Technical Supplement*, Rochester, Minnesota, published by CALLERLAB, 1991

Damon, S. Foster, *The History of Square Dancing*, Barre, Massachusetts: Barre Gazette, 1957.

Durlacher, Ed, *Honor Your Partner*, New York, New York: The Devin-Adair Company, 1949.

Gotcher, Les, *Les Gotcher's Textbook of American Square Dancing*, La Puente, California: Les Gotcher Enterprises, 1961

Holden, Ricky & Litman, Lloyd, *Instant Hash*, Cleveland, Ohio: published by the authors, 1962.
LOC# 60-15655

King, Jay, *The Fundamentals of Calling*, Lexington, Massachusetts: published by the author, 1968.

Lovett, Benjamin B. *Good Morning*, Dearborn, Michigan: The Dearborn Publishing Co., 1926.

Michl, Ed, *Build Your Hash*, Coshocton, Ohio, published by the author, 1963.

Osgood, Bob, Editor, *Year Books of Square Dancing* (Several), Los Angeles, California: Sets in Order Square Dance Publishers, 1954 - 1962.

Osgood, Bob, *The Caller Text - The Art and Science of Calling Square Dances*, Los Angeles, California: Compiled from *Sets in Order* magazine and organized by Bill Peters, 1985 LOC# 85-50621

Osgood, Bob, *The Caller Teacher Manual*, Los Angeles, California: *Square Dancing* magazine, 1983 LOC#82-63112.

Peters, Bill, *The Other Side of the Mike*, San Jose, California: published by the author, 1969

Putnam, Robert D., *Bowling Alone: The Collapse and Revival of American Community*, New York, New York: Simon & Schuster, Inc. 2000

Shaw, Lloyd, *Cowboy Dances,* Caldwell, Idaho: The Caxton Printers, Ltd 1939.

# ABOUT THE AUTHOR

Jim Mayo has been a part of modern square dancing from the beginning. As a teenager he made the transition from a traditional square dancer to a modern caller. He has shared in the founding of local caller associations in New England and in 1975 was elected the first Chairman of CALLERLAB, The International Association of Square Dance Callers. He has called and taught callers throughout North America and in Europe, Australia and New Zealand. He helped to write the book on training callers and has been a member of the CALLERLAB Board of Governors since its formation. He is one of a very small group of callers who have been actively calling for fifty years and are still at it.

Printed in the United States
1509300005B/187-279